CULTURE SHOCK!
Pakistan

**Karin Mittmann
Zafar Ihsan**

Graphic Arts Center Publishing Company
Portland, Oregon

In the same series

Australia	Hong Kong	Singapore	London at Your Door
Bolivia	India	South Africa	Paris at Your Door
Borneo	Indonesia	Spain	Rome at Your Door
Britain	Ireland	Sri Lanka	
Burma	Israel	Sweden	A Globe-Trotter's Guide
California	Italy	Switzerland	A Parent's Guide
Canada	Japan	Syria	A Student's Guide
Chile	Korea	Taiwan	A Traveller's Medical Guide
China	Laos	Thailand	A Wife's Guide
Cuba	Malaysia	Turkey	Living and Working Abroad
Czech	Mauritius	UAE	Working Holidays Abroad
Republic	Mexico	USA	
Denmark	Morocco	USA—The	
Egypt	Nepal	South	
France	Netherlands	Vietnam	
Germany	Norway		
Greece	Philippines		

Illustrations by Aktar Shah
Photographs by Karin Mittmann
Cover photographs from Photobank/Singapore

© 1991 Times Editions Pte Ltd
Reprinted 1995, 1996, 1998

This book is published by special
arrangement with Times Editions Pte Ltd
Times Centre, 1 New Industrial Road, Singapore 536196
International Standard Book Number 1-55868-059-4
Library of Congress Catalog Number 90-085616
Graphic Arts Center Publishing Company
P.O. Box 10306 • Portland, Oregon 97296-0306 • (503) 226-2402

All rights reserved. No part of this publication
may be reproduced, stored in a retrieval system,
or transmitted, in any form or by any means,
electronic, mechanical, photocopying, recording
or otherwise, without the prior permission of
the copyright owner.

Printed in Singapore

CONTENTS

FOREWORD

I once called Pakistan 'A castle with a thousand doors', for one can enter it from many sides, and once one has lived in it one discovers the same reality reflected in innumerable small mirrors of different colours. The thousand doors can be seen in the variety of languages and traditions, from the elegant, classical Urdu to the sweet Sindhi, the powerful lively Punjabi, the strong songs in Pashto and ballads in Balochi.

Although comparatively new as a political state, Pakistan's roots stretch much further back than colonial India and its fascinating archaeological sites, to the vibrant Harappa culture of the fourth millenium BC with its Buddhist, Greek, Hindu and Muslim elements.

Having lived in Pakistan for some 35 years, Karin Mittmann knows it and loves it, and any critical remarks are born out of love and deep feeling for the people and their values. In a friendship that has now lasted nearly 30 years I owe her unforgettable insights into the life of modern Pakistan, which supplement my own experiences as an interpreter of classical Pakistani and Indo-Muslim culture.

I do hope that the reader will gain a positive picture of the country and will begin to love it in spite of the difficult moments. Pakistan is a country that repays amply the visitor's patient attempt to understand it, and in the course of time one is drawn into the atmosphere of friendship and warmth.

I hope that *Culture Shock Pakistan* will serve as a fine and useful introduction into Pakistani life, and wish it and its readers every success.

Annemarie Schimmel
Professor of Indo-Muslim Culture, Harvard University

INTRODUCTION

Nobody can stay indifferent to Pakistan. It is like a watershed: this way or that way. Either foreigners reject it outright: no discos, no dancing or joy; women are hardly visible in the streets, no smiles. Or it grows on them and becomes a factor for the rest of their lives.

Pakistan is a country of extremes. It has the highest mountains, and the deepest seas. It has the most fertile plains and the biggest deserts. There are landscapes of moonlike barrenness from which come the juiciest fruits. It has snow, and 150 days of uninterrupted heat in a year. It knows the Seven Years of Drought — as well as monsoon floods that inundate thousands of villages most summers. It holds ever increasing masses of hungry people, as well as those who are — or have become — exceedingly rich; the greatest materialists next to the most pious, mystical souls in plenty. It can show a face of immense tolerance and, the next moment, the grimace of deadly hate. It has the strictest code of honour and religious rules and commits the most heinous crimes.

It is not a country for lightweights. Think of the majestic Himalayan mountains at whose feet the country sprawls: this is its mood. Even its beauty is grave or mighty.

Culture shock is certainly experienced by all who visit Pakistan for the first time. The customs, climate, language and foodstuffs are completely different from what they are used to at home. But with a little help and effort, you can adapt to what Pakistan has to offer; with a few essential tips on etiquette and customs you can avoid causing offence and instead bring great pleasure; by delving a little deeper and understanding more of the Pakistani's approach to work you can be a more successful employer; all these and more practical hints and advice are given in this book.

Chapter One

THE PAKISTANI PEOPLE

Although its cultural roots date back to the third millenium BC, Pakistan is a young state, formed in 1947 by the division of India. The movement for a separate Muslim homeland was the idea of the poet and philosopher Allama Iqbal in the 1930s. The movement itself was ably led by the lawyer Mohammad Ali Jinnah, who, together with the Hindu leader Mahatma Gandhi, succeeded by political acumen in achieving independence from British rule. It was Jinnah who subsequently really pressed the issue of a separate homeland for Muslims and achieved it in the form of the new state — Pakistan.

The clauses of the division of India provided that areas with a Hindu majority should form India and Muslim dominated areas should become Pakistan. Accordingly, Pakistan consisted originally of two wings, East and West Pakistan, with the huge area of 1600 kilometres of Indian terrority between them. East Pakistan comprised the area of East Bengal and West Pakistan was formed from the provinces of Sindh, Punjab, Baluchistan and the North West Frontier Province. The only common bond between the two wings was the Islamic religion.

In 1971, East Pakistan revolted and became independent. It is now known as Bangladesh. Since 1971, West Pakistan has been known as Pakistan. In the west and north, two Muslim states are Pakistan's neighbours, Iran and Afghanistan. In the east lies India and to the south the waves of the Indian Ocean lap the shore over several hundred kilometres.

The Land

There are four major geographical zones in Pakistan. The great highlands that border the north-west with their beautiful snow-capped mountains, swaying pine forests and lush green valleys form a paradise for tourists and trekkers from all over the world. The forbidding arid plateau of Baluchistan borders Iran in the west. In the south-east is wasteland and the Thar desert. And finally, the valley area of the Indus and its tributaries extends centrally from the north to the south of the country.

The most densely populated areas are along the mighty Indus river and its tributaries. The Indus enters Pakistan near Skardu high up in the rugged mountains. When it enters the plains, it spreads and becomes the father-river. In its course, it is joined by other great rivers, first the Kabul river in the west, followed by the Jhelum, Chenab, Ravi and Sutlej rivers towards the east and south.

The Climate

The climate is either arid or semi-arid. The Thar desert receives less than 13 centimetres of rain annually. In the central part of Pakistan the summer temperatures are around 45° C and reach 50° C on 'hot' days in the shade. All the land at the foot of the mountains from Peshawar to Lahore has cold winters; while the sunny midday is lovely, the night temperature may go below freezing point in January and, in the mountains of course, sub-zero temperatures are normal. Karachi has an all year average of 33° C maximum and 26° C minimum, but the temperature may vary by 20° in a single day. The winters in Sindh are quite mild.

The Monsoon

The monsoon winds that come from the Bay of Bengal reach up to the Indus where they unload their last, dying force. Lashing rains and heavy clouds reduce the temperature for some hours or days. When the sun breaks through, the steaming world around you may have 90 to 100% humidity at 40° C! It's a sauna but with your clothes on. People are irritable, everything is sticky, you drip from eyebrow to knees, and to work in a non-air-conditioned environment is a test for your nerves and heart. The season happens during July and August.

The extreme poverty, contrasting starkly with neighbouring extreme wealth, can be shocking to the westerner but is accepted as the status quo in Pakistan. This is partly because rarely has anyone in authority acted to improve the lot of the poor; partly too it is the result of the religious outlook whereby a poor man accepts his lot as Kismet, the will of God. Hence the attitude a visitor frequently meets is that people hardly ever say 'no' to you; but instead will 'hope' or 'be confident' that something will happen.

Within the echelons of the poor a mini class system has developed, whereby an underclass of slum-dwelling or rough sleeping casual labourers is stepped over by prospective employers in favour of choosing from the ranks of those used to the idea of working regular hours for a living.

THE DIFFERENT RACES

The great variety of races from dark skinned, or negroid, to the very fair and blue eyed; from hook-nosed to slant eyed; from high cheek-bones to long, narrow features is the next most noticeable feature of the Pakistanis. Invasions and migrations have played a great part in the forming of the major ethnic groups which are not reconciled to the idea of living under a common denominator. The last foreign rulers, the British, settled a great number of people in the Punjab; and at the time of partition a vast migration took place; Pakistan gave up 3 million Hindus and received 5 million Muslims. The main movement took place in the Punjab.

Today, there are five major ethnic groups in Pakistan. They are the Punjabis, the Pathans, the Sindhis, the Mohajirs, and the Balochis. Most of them are simply called after the name of the province they live in: the Punjabis inhabit Punjab (*panch* = five, *ab* = water — the land of the five rivers), the Sindhis, Sindh. The Pathans live in the North West Frontier Province and the Balochis live in the mountains and valleys of rugged Baluchistan. The Mohajirs are the people who migrated to Pakistan from central and southern India at the time of partition. There are many other smaller groups such as the Brahuis, the Gujeratis, the Chitralis, the Kashmiris and many more.

The Punjabis

The major groupings of the Punjabis claim descent from the Aryans. They constitute the majority of the population of Pakistan (63%) and have great influence in the country's political, military and social life. The Punjab is the most fertile region of the country and the Punjabis are consequently traditional farmers, or artisans. They are by and large tall and wheatish in complexion. They speak Punjabi, the old literary language of the area. It has several local dialects by which people recognise each others' home town or district. The men's traditional dress is a shirt worn over a long wrap called a *dhoti*. A turban is a must for the self respecting man. The women mostly wear the *shalwar kamis*, the wide trousers and long shirt which are worn by almost all Pakistani women.

The majority of Punjabis live in the rural areas and follow the centuries' old judicial and village administrative system of the Panchayat (panch = five, the fiver). This is a panel of five village elders who settle any disputes. It is only in cases where a decision is not acceptable that the matter goes to the court. However, this fine democratic self administrative system is now slowly dying out.

The Punjabis can be either extremely easy going, or fierce. They are traditionally very hospitable. They have a lot of folklore tradition, and they believe in saints, taboos and mystics. They will first go to a herbal medicine man, a *hakim*, or a saint, to cure an illness and to the doctor as the last resort. They pray at shrines and women who have not had children for a good part of their married life actually give their first born male child to the keepers of the shrines to become their disciples. They strongly believe in fate, and the failure of a crop or any other tragedy is borne with the stoicism of the knowledge that it was inevitable. On the other hand, a good crop or the good luck of an offspring is celebrated with gusto and community participation.

The ancient saints and mystics of the Punjab, like the ones of Sindh, have not only provided spiritual solace to the people but have also been a source of folklore music. *Heer Ranja* (the names of the hero and heroine) is perhaps the most popular of the ancient folklore tales. It is, like all of them, a love story and is sung without the accompaniment of an instrument. And a good singer can, every time, hold his listeners spellbound with the power of the poetry and the tune. The heroes of these great mystical epics, through their sufferings for the beloved, sublimate their love into the love of God. But the more popular songs that abound in the Punjab are sung at the time of the harvest and other traditional rural festivities. The most popular folkdance is the 'Bhangra', a circle dance in which both men and women participate.

The Pathans

This race also claims Aryan descent; some scholars however believe they are the lost tribe of Israel and in fact, the features of many Pathans, fierce and hook-nosed, lend support to this theory. Other theories add to the disputes. The Pathans fall into two groups, the tribal Pathans who live in the rugged mountains on both sides of the Pakistan-Afghan border, and the settled Pathans, the agriculturists. The tribal Pathans are tall, fair and fierce by feature and carriage. They carry arms from their early teens. The women are equally strongly built. They age fast, maybe because of the hardships that they have to endure. To fetch water in the tribal area may mean a march of many kilometres with several clay vessels on their heads. Their lands are barren and they make a living by being shepherds, smugglers and arms makers.

A Pathan at his best is next to none in appearance.

11

There are many tribes of Pathans, or Pakhtoons. The largest and famous ones are the Afridis, the Khattaks, the Waziris and the Yusufzais. Each of the major tribes falls into several smaller groupings. Living in the social formation of tribes has left them with a conservative attitude towards development and reform which is, therefore, much slower there than in the settled areas. For some years, a certain tribe has resisted the building of a government road through their territory and battles have even been fought over it. The result is a stalemate.

In their warrior-style and tall, handsome appearance Pathans are fascinating to meet. They are some of the best marksmen in the world. The British fought several big battles against them but never managed to subjugate them. The Khyber Pass is full of plaques commemorating the battles the British regiments fought there against them. Even the railway line that the British managed to lay from Peshawar to Landikotal in the middle of the Khyber Pass was known as the 'silver line', because everyday the British would lay a stretch of line and at night the Pathans would steal it to make arms.

They are led by tribal chiefs who are the ultimate authority and law which everyone in the tribe has to follow. Policy matters are discussed in the tribal chief's 'grand *jirga*', their parliament. This spirit has developed a certain democratic attitude that has prevented feudalism from running into excesses among the settled, agricultural Pathan landlords. This group of Pathans lives in the fertile upper Indus valley area of Mardan, Swabi and Peshawar, also in the dry southern parts of the Frontier Province around Bannu and Dera Ismail Khan. They are agriculturists. They have, by and large, preserved the character of tribal tradition, but the social structure of tribalism has given way to village style life. Their disputes are settled by their feudal lords. Often, they stick to the moral code of severe tribal morality: a tooth for tooth; an eye for eye; overwhelming hospitality.

Honour has the highest value: if a son meets the daughter of a neighbour, both are shot — by their fathers. Their women live mostly indoors and the tribal women always wear a wide and long rough cotton dress over the baggy shalwar. It is rare that a man sees his bride before marriage. A typical Pathan never walks with his wife or other female members of his family side by side. He will always walk in front and the women follow him in single file.

The Sindhis

The Sindhis are tall, slim and dark, with large eyes and mostly bearded. They dress in the usual shalwar kamis with the addition of a red cloth slung over their shoulder, the *ajrak*. They wear a cloth cap on their head which is embroidered and has many tiny mirrors stitched into it. Their caps prove the skill of their women at needle-work and embroidery. The traditional ajrak has different designs. Each tribe of Sindh has its own pattern which is woven into the ajrak. It is a piece of cloth about 2 metres long and 60–90 centimetres wide. It is hand-dyed in the traditional way from vegetable dyes and cow-dung. They speak Sindhi which has, through the intermediary language of Seraiki, a certain similarity to Punjabi.

The Sindhis only turned to systematic agriculture quite recently, when the extensive canal system was laid. Therefore, they are young agriculturists and old hunters. It is mostly the Hindu section of the Sindhi population that hunts in the riverine jungle of this province. It has left them rather poor, and agriculture, too, has only recently started to yield at a much greater potential. Land reforms by several governments have, by and large, failed. Feudalism there is generally oppressive. The landlord wields great social and political power. His money has won him a seat in the parliament — and nothing much changes. This last situation holds good for the whole of the country.

The women dress in the traditional shalwar kamis with very colourfully embroidered shirt-fronts. They, too, are strict about *purdah*, living behind the veil. Most of them are Muslims but the largest Hindu population of Pakistan also lives in Sindh. The urban Hindu is mostly a businessman or money-lender. The Sindhis are deeply steeped in mysticism and are therefore not renowned for being hard-working.

Sindh had an all Hindu population before its rulers were overthrown by the Muslims. Even now, when they greet each other, they do so by clasping their hands together like the Hindu *namaste*. Their old folk literature and music is highly developed and mostly of a mystical nature. Small wonder that their greatest and most popular poet was a mystic and saint of Sindh. His mausoleum is in Bathai in lower Sindh where thousands of worshippers arrive daily to pray and find solace.

The Mohajirs

The only common thread among the immigrants to Pakistan who are called Mohajirs (refugees) is that they are Urdu speaking. Although Urdu is the national language, each province or ethnic group speaks its own language or vernacular. Most of them are addicted to the betel nut and chewing of the betel leaf, or *pan*. On first sight you may think that the person is bleeding from his gums and lips as pan stains the mouth a reddish-brown. The Mohajirs are mostly industrial workers, clerks and businessmen. Numerically, they are the most educated class. Most of them have come from the states of United Provinces (U.P.) and Hyderabad, and later also from Bihar in India. They are generally dark and of fine-boned, medium height. Their women often wear the sari or long wide dresses depending where they originally come from.

Most of the Mohajir population is settled in Karachi where they constitute over 70% of the population as Karachi is the only large port of the country and the centre of business and industry. Being Muslims, they mostly came to Pakistan at the time of partition. They are shrewd businessmen and mostly keep their enterprise in the form of a family business. They have a very tightly-knit family system. Many close relatives with their families live in different sections of the same, large family house. Although they are clever traders they generally do not invest their money. They suffered greatly during the turmoil of partition and still feel insecure. They have therefore grouped themselves into a social and political block that wields considerable influence in Karachi.

The Balochis

The Balochis are partly Pathans and speak Pushto. There is hardly any difference between a Pathan from the North West Frontier Province and one from Baluchistan, as they are of the same Indo-Aryan race. If anything, the Balochis are even tougher and stronger than the ones of the northern tribes due to the extremes of climate and rough geophysical conditions. They are semi-nomadic. Several clans have moved down to Sindh and settled there as farmers like the Talpurs, the last dynasty of Sindh, who are originally Balochis. In the barren mountains only 11 people live per square kilometre, which has made administration of these unruly tribes with their forceful internal tribal organisation very difficult. The British felt it as acutely as later governments. Theft of cattle was an honorable deed of bravery, and until recently, a Balochi may have been introduced to you as 'the most famous cattle thief of the area'.

For the rest, there are some 250,000 Brahuis who inhabit Baluchistan who are probably the remnants of the Dravidian Mohenjo-daro culture. Their language is Dravidian. They are likewise, nomadic farmers but many of them have settled in the irrigated Sindh areas.

COMMON THREADS

Having discussed the differences among the major ethnic groups of Pakistan, we should also know what they have in common. First of all, there is the religion. All legal, social and cultural life finds its roots in Islam and is basically followed by all. Differences are offshoots of regional or ethnic influences. The Urdu language is, among the semi-educated and educated classes, another common factor.

Pakistanis are by nature rather stern. If at all, it is the Punjabi who laughs most easily. The heavy body of tradition often does not allow the development of progressive thinking. The glorification of personalities and events of years or ages gone by on the television screen makes the programmes often dull for a critical and forward-looking person; there is rarely a thrust into the future.

All groups believe in the joint family system and it is generally only the beginning of industrialisation and consequent job opportunities elsewhere that may force a young man to live away from his clan. The joint family system is a source of strength, for the Pakistani seldom marries outside his family. The husband and wife may often be first cousins or uncle and niece or any other mixed relatives. You will also smile when, as you often will, you hear a grown up woman address a small schoolboy in the formal manner of calling relatives, with the appellation 'uncle'.

Chapter Two

PAKISTAN — A MUSLIM STATE

Pakistan was founded in the name of Islam; it is the state religion.

RELIGIOUS SENTIMENTS AND PRACTICES

The devout Muslim is bound to pray five times a day; observe the strict fast of Ramadan; refrain from eating pork or drinking alcohol; and one day in his life should make the pilgrimage to Mecca, known as the 'Haj'.

Prayer

For his five daily prayers, the devout Muslim, wherever he is, will kneel down and perform the required ritual. For the five prayers of

17

the day, different numbers of obeisances are prescribed. After thorough ablutions, they are performed barefoot on a clean mat facing Mecca. Nobody should pass in front of a praying person.

Women do not say their prayers in public and only very few mosques are open to Muslim women to pray in. They pray in the silence of their bedrooms instead.

Ramadan

The month of fasting, Ramadan, is strictly observed by most adult Muslims. From before sunrise until the moment after sunset no food, drink, taste, dust or whatever other substance may pass the lips. At summer temperatures of over 40° C this is no small thing — on top of the workload. However, national production drops by 30% during Ramadan. One may earn less, go to the office late, be exhausted by the afternoon — nothing matters; the fast must be kept.

The Islamic calendar goes by the moon cycle, therefore Ramadan also occurs during the cool season after every 36 years.

After the *muezzin*, the mosque attendant, has given the *azan*, the prayer call from the mosque for the evening prayer, the Muslim will follow the example of the prophet and break fast with a date and water before going to the mosque for prayers. After that begins the feasting to which the food stalls in the bazaar (which double in number during the month of fasting) are eloquent witness. One may nibble away at titbits till bedtime; and at around 3 in the morning the housewife is up again to prepare a hot pre-sunrise meal!

Pork and Alcohol

A Muslim does not eat pork. He also does not drink. While there are plenty of substitutes for pork, there is none for Scotch. The answer lies behind the four walls of home where the state, which punishes the offence of drinking, cannot peep; for the rest, he prays for God's forgiveness.

The Haj

Once in his life time it is obligatory upon a Muslim to perform Haj, the pilgrimage to the holy city of Mecca. After successful completion of the exhausting rituals there, the pilgrim adopts the title 'Haji'. A man thus introduced, will be addressed with 'Haji Sahib' (Mr Pilgrim). Women are 'Hajianis' but are not addressed as such.

Young and Old

Before a boy reaches adolescence he must be circumcised. A dead man may not be cremated but is buried as he is. A menstruating woman may not pray nor fast. These are the most important dogmas which the average Muslim observes quite strictly. There are innumerable other practices which undergo minor changes with time and place.

Headcovers

When a verse from the Koran is recited at the beginning of a formal function or serious undertaking, or prayer takes place anywhere, or the azan, the call for prayers is heard, it is best if women cover their heads just like local women do. It is advisable to carry a scarf along at all times, although there is great tolerance and acceptance of other peoples' customs.

Halal Meat

Animals are invariably slaughtered by cutting the jugular vein and uttering the words 'Allah-u-Akbar', God is greatest. Meat that is not treated this way may be refused by strict Muslims; and when they go abroad, they might even restrict their diet to a vegetarian one.

Gratitude

One should not expect to be thanked for a gift or kind deed, since everything comes from Allah, the Merciful, and man just executes

His orders. Some modern, educated city dwellers may be an exception to this rule. And when someone has done well in an examination or got a job, he attributes his success to Allah's mercy. And he often offers a thanksgiving sacrifice 'Sadka' in the form of alms or gift for the poor.

Dress

Women must keep their heads covered with the *dupatta*, the fine, mostly beautiful veil, particularly in the presence of elders (modern, urban women often ignore the dupatta) and keep their eyes cast down and only speak in answer to a question. When going out, many women wear the *burquah*, the black or white cloak that totally shrouds the person, though in recent times this has come to be identified with low, middle and poorer classes.

The Muslim shaves his body hair. He mostly eats with his fingers, some refuse to use cutlery as being an instrument of non-believers; they sometimes wear the Pakistani shalwar kamis (wide trousers and shirt) as a protest against the 'westernized, tradition-alienated corrupt Muslim' of modern, sophisticated tastes. This is to be seen as an attempt to establish and confirm their cultural identity within the context of Islam.

Customs and Rituals

Customs and rituals occupy a dominant place in the heart, mind, time and purse of every Muslim.

Dogs are largely considered unclean. There may be servants who refuse to brush a pet dog. In the course of time, they might learn otherwise; if not, there is no way to force them. Only a few urban families keep dogs as pets, but many keep huge dogs as guard dogs.

Marriages abound in rites. Step by step the several, lengthy celebrations move from one *rasm* (ritual) to the next and the next... (see page 109). Similarly, funerals. The last rites are performed strictly in accordance with the Holy Book.

It is customary to precede a formal function or serious undertaking with the phrase 'Bismillah' — in the name of God — and acknowledge a good outcome with 'al-Hamdulillah' — praise be to God.

Religious minded men follow the example of the *mullah*, the priest, and sport a beard of any length. Many wear the white skullcap which is used for prayer, on their heads all the time. Due to centuries of proximity, many Hindu rites and customs have been adopted by Muslims: the dowry system which weighs heavily on all parents, the shaving off of a newborn's hair and the burning of perfumed sticks at holy places are examples of such rituals.

SUFIS, SHRINES AND SPIRITS

Sufis

The Holy Book reveals God's laws to show the complete way of life. It is like the trunk of a tree through which the lifeline runs. From there, it blossoms out into the deepest and glowing perceptions of nearness to and love of God: into Sufism, Islamic mysticism of which there are many schools.

Pakistan has abounded in mystic teachers, preachers, poets and singers through the centuries, mostly in Sindh. Some of the old Sindhi or Punjabi mystics have produced sublime verses which compare with the best in world literature. The topic of the love for God is brought near to the common man in the form of poetry and folktales which are recited and sung by almost everybody. There is hardly a person who does not know and love the stories of 'Sohni-Maiwal' or 'Heer-Ranja'.

Shrines

People perform pilgrimages to the burial places of saintly persons over which elaborate mausoleums have been built. The villager

21

expresses his love of the saint and God, by using different colours for the mosque design, and for the shrine or shrine cover, with mirror pieces and other embellishments.

In Multan, Uchh and Sewan Sharif are some of the finest mausoleums that Muslim architecture has produced. Many thousands of other saintly persons are buried and venerated thus — which village would not like to have its own saint? And often, there is more than one. People come in thousands to pray there and whisper their secret wishes to the saint; they often hang padlocks to the grill of the shrine, to be opened only after the wish has been granted. Desperate women, under threat of divorce, fervently pray for a son or fertility. There are often more women than men around a shrine. And if then a son is born, the saint's spiritual powers are acclaimed far and wide and attract even more pilgrims.

Every saint has his *Urs,* the annual festival. Up to 200,000 believers may come to the famous shrines of old mystics and saints, often travelling barefoot through deserts and heat, suffering from hunger and thirst. Such spiritual fervour is a unique and deep experience.

Spirits

The belief in the spiritual powers of a dead or living saintly person, in evil and good spirits, reminds us of the Middle Ages. An evil spirit can stunt a child's growth, render the buffalo infertile and the land barren; the good spirit may cure a disease, pass exams and get you jobs, and the like. The word of a good spirit is used as weapon against the evil eye. Holy men write Koran verses for people which they carry along or wear on their body like amulets. Drivers very often hang black cloth flags on their car fenders and fix a plate with Koranic verses or paint the magic number 867 on their cars — against the evil eye of an accident.

The 'evil eye' is the concretisation of fear in the face of good luck which may evoke the jealousy of the gods. It is one of the very early fears of man found amongst all peoples. To protect from the evil eye you tie black cloth to the fenders of vehicles, speak holy verses and wear amulets. A new-born baby is protected by uttering holy verses from the Koran into his ear, so that he becomes a Muslim. It may bring bad luck and might evoke the evil eye, to congratulate a pretty child on good looks.

The deep religious feelings of the Pakistani Muslim manifest themselves in many forms and on all occasions. It is his mainstay in his poverty, in disease and calamity, which he bears with stoic acceptance of God's will. He must truly be admired for his strength of faith.

RELIGIOUS FESTIVALS

Eid Ul Fiter or Chhoti Eid (Small Eid)

The two great religious festivals are the two Eids. On the first of the two Eid festivals, the young of a family receive a new set of clothes

Festivals are mostly introduced by congregational prayer.

and monetary gifts. Beggars are not turned away empty handed from the gate, companies normally give a bonus to their employees, and your household servants expect a generous monetary gift commensurate with the master's financial standing. They are often given one or two days off. The Christian servants should not feel left out of the celebrations entirely and may be given a smaller monetary compensation. (The reverse happens at Christmas.)

The first, the 'Small Eid', celebrates the end of Ramadan, the fasting month. It is impatiently awaited by fasters and non-fasters alike: children and young girls are dressed in bright new shalwar kamis (wide trousers and shirt), colourful glass bangles decorate the arms of young and old, on palms a filigree design is traced with henna, a red dye, and shopping for new shoes is a long awaited excitement by itself.

After 28 days of fasting, all eyes scan the western horizon for the new moon, in case it is in such a phase that it will show and thus shorten the fast by one day. Sometimes, this does happen, mostly in the western part of the country, which results in two 'Eids' on two different days in the west and east of the country. The phantom and hair-thin crescent is a miracle to the eye. From that moment on for nearly a week you wish everybody 'Eid Mubarak' (congratulations on Eid) and the celebrations get under way. The women cook, stitch, sing, and clean through most of the night.

Early in the morning, the man of the house and his male offspring go to the mosque for Eid prayers after which men and children visit neighbours, friends and relatives; women are mostly too busy entertaining them to be able to go out on the first day of Eid. Very few mosques make arrangements for women to say their Eid prayers there. Most pray at home before the final preparations for the day begin. Food is central to the 'Small Eid' and in villages bears dance and merry-go-rounds swing with loud music on the village ground. You send Eid greetings cards to friends and take boxes of sweetmeats when you visit them on this occasion.

Eid Ul Azha or Bari Eid

Ten weeks after the 'Small Eid' comes the 'Big Eid'. This is the occasion when you slaughter an animal as Abraham did when God forbade him to sacrifice his son. Each family slaughters a male goat, sheep or calf. There may not be enough money in the kitty to buy a bicycle for the son to reach the school several kilometres away, but the sacrifice is a proud MUST.

On the Eid day itself men again get ready for the prayer in the mosque. This time, there is no confusion about moon or no moon, as Eid ul Azha falls on the 10th day after the new moon. When the men return home from prayers they try to arrive with a butcher in tow; for now the sacrifice has to be enacted. The butcher kills the

25

animals with the word 'Bismillah' and cuts the jugular veins. The streets fill with the blood of the sacrificial animals and their innards overflow from every garbage bin or dump. The cities' civic authorities give early warnings and instructions, but the waste still lies around for days. The hides are collected by mosques and sold for charitable purposes.

The sacrificial meat is divided into three portions, one for the needy, one for friends and relatives, and one for the household itself. Servants and the young ones of a family go around with covered trays distributing plates full of pieces of raw meat and receive the same amount back in return. Meat is sent to orphanages and is given to beggars who stand at your gate. Pakistanis are meat lovers and spend the next two days eating meat cooked in a variety of ways.

Although the celebration holds greatest signficance, the excitement is not quite as great; may be, it is too close to the Small Eid for most families to afford another set of clothes or gifts. Servants normally get a smaller amount and the mailman, the milkman, the telegram-man and so on will wish you a happy Eid and give you a letter which he probably kept in his pocket for days in the hope that on this occasion you have the right answer for his expectant eyes. It's wise to collect many ten and fifty rupee notes before the Eids.

Muharram

On the 10th day of the month of Muharram — the first month in the Islamic calendar year — falls the anniversary of the death of Hussein who was killed defending the true values of Islam some 1300 years ago. There are 10 days of mourning, and then the Shias, the second largest sect in Islam, who split from the Sunnis over this issue and are the followers of Hussein, hold huge public processions and commemorate Hussein's sufferings by self flagellations. Anyone with strong nerves may watch. Visitors are often offered seats on the balconies along the roads on which the procession passes. If you can

During the Muharram Procession young believers hit their backs with five sharp blades. Those who are exhausted are immediately replaced by others, all crying 'Ya Allah, Ya Hussein'.

stand the sight of blood streaming down backs that are beaten with a whip which has nails at its end, do go and take your cameras along.

Sunnis, the largest sect in Islam, also mourn the death of Hussein but in quiet ways. For 10 days all cinemas are closed, no music is heard and all entertainment comes to a standstill. No expatriate should give a party with or for Muslim friends or offend religious feelings by playing loud music at this time.

It is advisable to keep away from a few areas in Pakistan where, on this occasion, religious sentiments run too high and Sunni-Shia differences are fought out with rifles and knives. That happens sometimes in the north and north-western parts of the country.

Others

The birthday of the Prophet Mohammed is celebrated with prayers and the exchange of sweets cooked at home. The night of Mohammed's ascension is commemorated by lighting candles or oil lamps and offering prayers. All these festivals move around the year and always occur ten days earlier than in the previous year.

Islamic Law

As a result of colonial rule, the Sub-continent has been under British Law for centuries, although the tribal groups had, and still follow, their own law, the Pakhtoonwali. With independence and the new sense of Islamic nationhood, it became necessary to follow the Islamic Laws as given in the Holy Koran. But due to the many sects and their different interpretations of the holy texts, there is no uniform opinion as to what exactly Islamic Law is. As God's word cannot be tampered with, compromise is ruled out and each group considers its own version as the final word of God.

The government instituted the Council of Islamic Ideology whose task it is to find an interpretation that is acceptable to all groups. Since 1984, the Shariah Bill, the Islamic Law Bill, has been in existence. Islamic Law, for example, provides for cutting off the hand of a thief; but the few court verdicts giving this sentence could not be executed because doctors refused to carry them out.

Welfare Tax

The Zakat, the voluntary welfare contribution, is now deducted by state law automatically from all Muslim bank accounts, land holdings and shares. But the Shias do not pay the tax; they insist that they follow a different system. This has not yet been passed by parliament.

Death Penalty

Islamic Law provides for the dealth penalty for certain criminal offences. But mercy shown by the offended party is considered superior. Tribes settle their disputes by themselves; if a girl is dishonoured or a relative killed, revenge follows the evil-doer until he is killed; but also, the offended girl must be killed, as the family cannot live with their name thus shamed.

Religious Taboos

There are few religious taboos. By and large, great tolerance is shown to foreigners as they cannot be expected to know all do's and don'ts of the religion. However, a people that is so emotional about its religion can also be expected to react strongly if their religious sentiments are insulted. The rules are simple.

Discussions

Religion is discussed everywhere: on the bus, in shops, in offices, simply everywhere — discussed but never criticised. Note the difference.

You will please every Muslim if you show interest and ask him questions on Islam, its history, happenings and rituals, and mostly he will give you detailed and accurate information.

CLOTHES

In Pakistan, as generally in Muslim countries, it is wise to wear clothes that cover the legs and at least half the arm, particularly so when you enter a mosque, shrine, mausoleum or attend a religious function.

Women are advised not to wear tightly fitting clothes. Pakistani women's clothing is most comfortable, elegant and suits all climates. Women can get a fine cotton shalwar kamis outfit very cheaply. You need not wear the dupatta that comes with it, although it's beautiful, but you might keep it ready in your handbag as protection from dust, rain, heat, stares — or just to drape around yourself. But keep that for special occasions, in the bazaar it's meant to show your modesty.

Holy places must be entered barefoot. Take warm socks with you in winter on such sightseeing tours, as you don't get slippers at the gate. It will do no harm if you now put your dupatta over your head. You may take photos of any and all holy places although it is courteous to ask permission, but take care that you do not snap a passing woman by mistake!

RULES FOR RAMADAN

During the month of fasting, all restaurants are closed until sundown. People will not say anything but frown if, during this month, you should smoke, eat or drink in public. Only children are excepted, but exercise tact and courtesy: there is really no need to give them a biscuit in front of people whose stomachs are empty.

4- and 5- star hotels provide the normal food and meals to non-Muslim foreigners. On the national airline, PIA, everybody is asked whether he wants to eat his meal at normal times or at Ramadan times, although there is an exemption from fasting for those travelling.

Drink

The drinking of alcohol is prohibited in Islam. There are no shops selling liquor. Those who need it make it at home or have other channels of procurement. If you have no entitlement to import it or no other sources to buy it, you can get beer, whisky, gin and vodka (all locally made and quite good, the beer being very good) at the clubs (if you are a member) or at a 5-star hotel. For that, you need a permit. It carries the elaborate title: 'Permit under the Prohibition Order 1979 for the Purchase, Possession, Transport and Consumption of Intoxicating Liquors by a Foreigner or Tourist Holding a Valid Passport'. You can obtain one from the Excise Department in the cities.

Even a foreigner should never drink alcohol in public. Drinking is such a delicate issue that grown up men who do drink, will often not do so in their homes (it would render the home unclean), or in front of their elders (out of respect). And some never drink in front of the women of the house. The same often holds for smoking cigarettes.

Food

If you really cannot avoid offering pork at your party, in whatever form, you must clearly label the dish that contains it PORK. On no account should pork be placed on a dish containing other foodstuffs.

SECTS AND MINORITIES

There are over 70 Islamic sects in Pakistan; several are split into sub-sects. All of them fall under the two major groupings of Sunnis (who also include as dogmatic revelations the oral tradition of Mohammed's sayings) and the Shias.

Some of the larger sects are called Agha Khanis or Ismaelis, Wahabis, Memons and Boras. They mostly differ in aspects of interpretation of the Koran.

Minorities

The Ahmadis, also known as Kadianis, were a Muslim sect till 1974 when the government declared them a minority. In all practical matters, they follow the Koran.

Parsis

There are some Parsi families in Lahore and a small sized community in Karachi. They are descendants of old Persian Zoroastrians who, when persecuted, fled eastwards. They are a quiet, well educated and well-off community and are known for depositing their dead on high towers to be devoured by crows and vultures.

31

Hindus

After partition, only a few Hindus stayed back in the northern parts of Pakistan. In the South, in Sindh, there are several thousand Hindus who are mostly peasants and businessmen. Hindu temples can still be seen here and there but mostly they are crumbling from neglect.

Christians

The largest minority are the Christians. They are mostly former converts of low Hindu castes. Therefore, most of them are poor and perform humble jobs. Most of the sweepers are Christians.

The British, during the Raj, built fine churches in towns and cities which are now used by the Pakistani Christians. A few new churches have been added here and there.

Islam acknowledges the Jewish and Christian prophets. Christianity is 'of the Book'. A Muslim man may marry a Christian girl, but not vice versa. Muslims respect Jesus as a prophet and quite often, children have Christian names: Isa, Mariam, Yusuf...

By and large, the sects and minorities live peacefully side by side.

THE MOSQUE

The mosque is not only the Muslim place of worship but it also has social, educational and political functions.

All day through you will find men sitting alone or in small groups in the large mosque hall or courtyard engrossed in low-key conversation. Some just do not know where to go and look for company there. Mostly in the afternoon, small groups of children come there and receive instruction in the Holy Text and in Arabic, the language of the Koran. Due to the lack of primary schools and of teachers, some mosques now take over the function of elementary schools. Since in cities there are mosques every few hundred metres from each other, men often rush there for the prescribed five

Discipline and submission mark the ritual of formal prayer.

prayers a day. Mostly though, they perform the rituals wherever they are at the time of the azan.

The Azan

The azan is the call to prayer which the mosque attendant, the muezzin, traditionally performs from the top of one of the high minarets, the towers of a mosque. The lone voice from high up in the air pronouncing the powerful words in rhythmic intonation: 'In the name of God, the Almighty, the Merciful ... there is no other god but God ...' has a singularly elevating effect.

In modern times, the loudspeaker has taken over, a shrill metallic sound which has robbed the azan of its pristine beauty. Knowledgeable expatriates, when they look for a house, make sure it is not too close to a mosque or that its bedroom windows face away from it, in order to avoid being woken by the 3.30 a.m. azan.

The Friday midday prayer is the most important service of the week. A substantial number of men then flock to the mosque.

Before the prayer and ritual begin, most mullahs will hold a political oratory. They have never really praised any government for none has been Islamic enough.

The Mullah

There are degrees of Islamic scholarliness, but mostly the Islamic priest is referred to as the mullah. When addressed, he will be politely called 'Maulvi Sahib'. By and large the mullah lacks general education, and can be dogmatic and narrow minded. However, he wields vast power over his community, particularly in far flung and poor areas. His word there is revelation. And since Islam is a complete way of life including politics, the mullah preaches politics as well. The mullahs constitute a force that every government has to reckon with.

The mullah invariably grows a long beard. Other men who keep long beards must be considered persons of religious standing, often hajis. Many of them also wear a white skullcap during the day.

Mosque Architecture

The religious spirit of Islam has found its finest cultural expression in the construction of mosques. There are the graceful African ones; there are the incomparable Byzantine ones; there are the domed Persian ones. And Pakistan can boast of some of the finest.

The great Badshahi Mosque (Imperial Mosque) in Lahore is of royal dimensions and exquisite proportions. This Moghul mosque was considered the largest mosque in the world until the Shah Faisal Mosque in Islamabad was completed in 1986. The latter blends the Arabic tent shape with most modern architectural features in perfect harmony and grandeur. The hundreds of floral designs on the marble panels of Lahore's Wazir Khan Mosque are of the finest decorative styles — it is a cheerful mosque, while the Moghul period mosque in Thatta in southern Sindh breathes a mystical other-worldliness.

All mosques are open to visitors, but do not forget to take off

Young girls are taught from the Koran at home by female relatives.

your shoes at the gate. Do not visit wearing shorts. Women should preferably wear a long-sleeved dress, and should cover their heads with a shawl or handkerchief.

WOMEN AND RELIGION

The Pakistani woman is the real torch bearer of Islam in her own, quiet way: she prays in the silence of her home; she teaches her children the Koranic laws and instils in her daughters modesty and

35

acceptance of their fate; she teaches them to be obedient to the seniors; to bite their lips rather than cry; how to say the five prayers and how to fast. Women very frequently go to the shrines of holy men and fervently pray there. They send a meat dish to a poor person and give away saved coins and used clothes.

The most glaringly attired or emancipated modern women respond with their souls when it comes to religion. Deep faith in the Holy Scriptures gives them solace. Their lot here is not easy, much more difficult than men's. Surrendering to the will of God has filled many women with great spiritual strength.

The belief in the remedial powers of saints both buried and alive has given rise to a somewhat excessive reliance on external sources for help in cases of sickness, danger, misery and the like. Shrines are mostly crowded by women. Living 'Holy men' have sometimes exploited their faith. However, it is remarkable how effective the *ta'weez*, the talisman, can be: it may cure infertility, stunted growth because of the evil eye, or take away the deadly fever; each cure makes the shrine or holy man more famous. No wonder some unscrupulous people become 'holy men' as their profession! Evil and good spirits hover in plenty, not only in remote areas, and cancel each other's effectiveness. This is a great topic among women.

Chapter Three

ABOUT THE LANGUAGE

The Five All-Weather Words

You are standing on Pakistani soil. How do you communicate with the people of the land? The answer is simple. Equipped with just five words, and their wealth of meaning, you march along the Pakistani roads fearlessly.

Along the roads are very many simple villages with hospitable people. When you think you had enough of their friendly, giggly curiosity or of their strong, sweet tea, or you find that the offered food burns your tongue out of your mouth, come out with an energetic 'bus'. If, by a miracle, someone still insists, you just say 'bus, bus' (enough is enough) and you will notice the retreat. On the other side of the road are many beggars. If you find your generosity exploited beyond willingness you simply say a solid 'bus' to the crowd and march on.

'T'heek-hae' is your 'OK' when you have found the deal or the returned cash in order, the documents properly filled in, the food acceptable, the lodgings clean enough. Your dealer or host may ask you 't'heek hae?' and if you approve his offer, you answer with an affirmative 't'heek hae'. It concludes every deal followed by sighs of relief when liver functions and blood pressure levels return to normal.

Your first needs are those of survival. In the furnace temperature of summer, keep the word 'pani' right on the tip of your tongue. You utter it and you will very quickly be given the water you need. It is a fine Islamic tradition among pious people and some urban dwellers that they keep large earthen jars with a tin or plastic mug attached to them, outside their gate or wall — for everyone knows the consequences of dehydration. And, even at 45° C in the shade you will find the pitcher water always delightfully cool, and more wholesome than chilled water. So do not forget the word 'pani'. However, if your internal system is not equipped to deal with the multitudes of water insects and bacteria, you may end up in hospital, so, you may do better with 'cola', hardly a word to be learnt by foreigners, and you find these slim bottles everywhere.

If you are hungry, 'roti' is the magic word. *Roti* is bread, the collective term for the varieties of flat, round breadcakes. There are about a dozen delicious kinds of them, all cheap. And always safe to eat.

You may find a group of men squatting by the road side tearing chunks from the roti in their hands and dipping them into a reddish brew on a plate in the midst. They may gesture to you and say 'roti k'ha'o'. Roti here, means meal, and they invite you to share a meal with them. Although they are mostly poor, they will be delighted if you accept their invitation. Hopefully, you will be able to squat for the length of a meal. You might choose not to dip the bread chunks into the curry sauce on the plate if you do not like chillies, as this brew may bring tears to your eyes and revolt your stomach.

It is one of the finest Muslim traditions that, almost anywhere, you will be asked to join in a meal that is in progress. Without even thinking about it, everyone will eat a little less to make the roti go round — and feel pleasure in doing so. If, at the end of the meal you can produce a toffee, biscuit or cigarette from your knapsack to share with them, you will earn yourself great praise and life-long remembrance in the spirit of Islamic brotherhood. Their cultural sensibilities thus acknowledged, you may receive offers of help, hospitality and friendship. It takes little doing to find friends along the ups and downs of Pakistani roads.

By far the most unifying of all words of the over 300 languages spoken in this country is the word 'ách'ha'. Basically, it means 'good'; 'ách'ha hae' means 'this is good'. But this is its restricted, so to say, fettered meaning. You can set the word free and let it soar and achieve unimaginable depths and breadths of communication. Let us throw some light on them:

1. You enter Pakistan at an international airport. The immigration officer may point out that you need more signatures or stamps on your documents. When you have understood his point of view you signal it by a short 'ách'ha' which you may repeat after every sentence of his.

2. If somebody has been explaining to you the route to the nearest hotel for the last 10 minutes and by now you feel satisfied that, whichever road you take, they all lead to your hotel, and you also feel that you had enough of his generous help, you shoot a series of 'Ach'ha's' at him accompanied by serious nods of the head: all is clear, thank you.

3. If you want to enter into deeper levels of communication with the helpful person, you might want to show him your astonishment that so many roads lead to the hotel: you simply draw the last syllable to any length of the vowel 'a': 'ách'haaa; ách'haaah!' It also satisfies the person that you believe implicitly in him.

4. Another variation of the magic word lies in raising your voice to a short crisp question tone on the second syllable 'ách'haa?'. This, you say in answer to such assertion as: 'Wall Street has just collapsed,' or, 'Our buffalo has given birth to a three legged calf.' The drawl and the pitch of voice indicate that you are wonderstruck or incredulous.

5. A drab, short, repeated 'ách'ha' indicates you agree but without enthusiasm.

The miraculous Pakistani telephone system generally allows you to be an unnoticed witness to other people's conversations or to just one of the conversing partners. And, for the length of 10 minutes at least, you may hear the following:

'Ach'ha'	(that's fine with me)
'Ach'haa-ách'ha'	(I understand)
'Ach'hha?'	(really?)
'Ach'haa!'	(how wonderful)
'Aachch'h!'	(well!)
'Ach'hhaah!'	(I am shocked!)
'Ach'ha ách'haa'	(don't say any more — I know it any way)
'Ach'hah!'	(OK)
'Ach'hha?'	(that's all?)
'Aach'ha!'	(nothing more to tell, OK then, bye!)

THE LANGUAGES OF PAKISTAN

The many ethnic groups in Pakistan can also be distinguished by their different languages: the Punjabis speak Punjabi, the Sindhis Sindhi, the Balochis Balochi and the Pathans Pakhto (or Pashto). This list can be extended almost endlessly. Philologists say that there are over 300 dialects and languages spoken in the country today — and each is distinctly different from the other.

The Unifying Factor: Urdu

The problem of communication was felt acutely under early Moghul rule when soldiers could not communicate with other groups of soldiers and orders were not understood by many. A new common language evolved: Urdu, the word for army.

This amalgam consists of the local Hindi, Persian and Arabic. It answered the need of the time so well that, within one hundred years, Urdu was a literary language in which, even now, great works of prose and poetry are written. It is the official language and is taught in all schools. It is spoken in the north and south of the country, understood largely in India and as far west as the Emirates and some cities of Saudi Arabia. It would only be in the smaller villages that a traveller, Pakistani or foreigner, would not be understood if he addressed the inhabitants in Urdu.

Not all foreigners take the trouble to learn Urdu, since most city dwellers know at least some words of English — a fact which they love to prove to the foreigner. Most cooks know the names of the menus in English, ayahs know the English nursery rhymes by heart and traders proclaim their wares in English — even on their sign-boards. This is the legacy of 200 years of British rule.

While many have a little and some, an excellent command over this international language, it has generally given people an outlook on life that is worldwide and welcoming to foreigners.

The Sounds of Urdu

The easy part of the language is that it is phonetic. 'A' sounds like 'u' in 'but' or, if long, like 'a' in 'smart'. You speak the vowel 'i' like 'i' in 'sit' or, if long, the first 'e' in 'even'. 'E' is like 'e' in 'the'; 'o' as the English 'or' and 'u' like 'oo' in 'room'. The diphthong 'ae' sounds like 'a' in 'hat'. Vowel sounds are almost

41

identical with those of Latin or German.

A few consonants pose a problem. There are two, sometimes three different sounds to the letter 't', 'd' and 'r' which the western ear cannot easily hear even after years. All others are the same as in English with a few additions.

Some phonetic symbols introduced here will be followed throughout:

a	=	long a (or other vowel)
à	=	toneless vowel
ñ	=	nasal n
kh	=	like the German ch in 'ach' or 'doch' (or Loch Ness in Scotland)
k'h	=	'h', hardly audible, often follows a consonant. It helps establish a heavy vowel sound.
gh	=	like the French or German r
páni	=	emphasised syllable

Here are some of the most common courtesies and greetings.

Assalam aléikum	=	God's peace be with you (for all times of the day). The answer to it is
wa'al´éikum salam	=	and with you too
khodáh hafíz	=	God be with you; good bye
shúkri'a	=	thank you
bóhat shúkri'a	=	thank you very much
kya hal hae	=	how are you? The positive, expected answer is
T'heek hae	=	I am fine
ách'ha	=	good
bóhat ách-ha	=	very good

There is no real word for 'please' in Urdu; instead, the class-conscious society produced three different verb endings, applied to different classes of man which imply:

Káro!	=	Do it!
Káren!	=	Please do it!
Kár liji'eñ!	=	Would you please be so kind and do it.

42

Every Pakistani is happy when a foreign guest addresses him in his native language, even though it may only be a few words. The expatriate will feel the beneficial influence that the trouble of learning some words and phrases will have. Extending your hand is a gesture of goodwill; so much greater is the gesture of learning some Urdu words. You will feel good and reduce the culture shock. Moreover, the one step you have taken will earn you three steps of Pakistani goodwill. You lose nothing and gain a lot.

The Script

The script is difficult and is used in two different scriptural styles: Nask'h which developed in Arabia from the medieval kufi script; and Nastaleeq, the 'hanging Nask'h' which developed in 14th-century Persia. Although they are quite similar they require separate study. It is mostly the system of joining letters that makes the study of either style difficult and lengthy: most letters, but not all, appear only in part and that, too, in a different part depending on their use in the beginning, the end or in the middle of a word. Then, there are some homophones which the western ear can hardly perceive, but the script has two to three different letters for each: 't', 'd', 'r', 'k' and 'z'. It requires energetic pursuit and a lot of practice to be able to read or write adequately.

Luckily, the same British legacy has been kept alive in the writing of the language as well: road signs are often in English; Urdu and English are both the official languages; there are several English newspapers with a vast circulation and the radio and TV both offer several news bulletins in English.

Chapter Four

THE SOCIAL CIRCLE

The Pakistani has an uncomplicated social nature. Unless you are in a formal function, he or she will come forward to meet you. He, but mostly she, will tell a foreign lady at once how many sons she has and introduce her to the size and problems of her family and clan. She will then enquire about your family. I know some foreign women here who, though childless, have learnt how to avoid the pity and insistance of local people and, in order to be considered normal, reply that their son and daughter are studying abroad.

For a woman, your husband's income is the next issue of burning interest, and pressing questions are asked about this with no hesitation. The more you oblige, the more pressure will follow. In order to divert their enquiry, you could reply 'ten dumplings' or 'ten cubes' using any word that might sound like a currency, then explain that you don't know about its rupee value but that it is enough for you all to live on. You will hear such questions without any introductions in small towns, within the old city walls — wherever social groups have escaped the sophistications and courtesies of modern urban living.

Even there, the code is simple. One age-old tradition has stayed alive among all circles: the elders must be respected at all cost; and first the men, followed by women. They are greeted first, others are introduced to them. They are seated on the best chairs, and get their tea or meal first. Only in tradition-conscious circles would they alone ask questions and accept the answers and not a word more; the modern old gentleman or lady will be pleased by your interest in them, even if it is through a translator.

Handshakes

Men shake hands; friends embrace; Pathans embrace both left and right. The greetings are invariably hearty and honest. Introductions follow the European pattern. In business circles, it has become customary to exchange name-cards; titles and academic distinctions go quite a way in establishing your credentials. While the Pakistani is formal in his address and does not skip the Sahib, or Mr or Mrs, some of the younger generation have adopted the American way of informality by asking and using first names.

The master normally extends his hand to a lower employee or servant on first meeting him and when wishing him well on days of religious celebration, but otherwise not.

For women from anywhere except other Asian countries, Pakistani customs are a culture shock. Traditionally women do not shake hands with men, and even the recent first woman prime minister used the orthodox style of greeting, and did not shake hands with men. This has actually never been done in the Muslim society here; but there has been a tendency towards it among modern thinkers. Some of the independent thinking women might stretch out their hand for a greeting, and a foreign woman may do so without hesitation. But a man should never be the first to extend his hand to a lady. There are women who interact with men in business or social life like women in the western world; but they will not expect to be jovially slapped on the shoulder or hugged.

Flattery

Western women, who in the west are normally hardly taken note of by men, or only occasionally hear a word of courteous attention or appreciation, are often overwhelmed by the flights of imagination and exotic dreamlands and promises that men shower upon them during a social evening. But beware! Enjoy the words, but make no promises. Western films and magazines have given rise to a negative image of a western woman who is freely available to everyone. It takes some practice to speak with that tone of friendly authority that carries the message that you want to convey and yet be totally polite, charming and gracious.

Gentlemen

Some gentlemen can be extremely courteous and show a lady respect and all civilities. But when you meet them in the company of their village elders, fathers, brothers or friends, you can often hardly recognise their behaviour: they will let you trail last in the line, and not notice whether you find a seat or receive a cup of tea. They are now overacting in the face of the clash with their traditional world and are afraid of being ridiculed by old intimates or boyhood friends; while their elders might even deplore their alienation from traditional values. This is the clash in the minds of progressive thinking Pakistanis and it would be harmful to you and to your relationship with them if you called them rude, unpolished or inconstant. They live under too many pressures and have yet to find their place in the modern way of life.

NAMES AND TITLES

The foreign visitor will certainly face a problem when it comes to names. They not only sound foreign but a person has normally more than one name and the foreigner does not know which one to use.

The Pakistani will introduce himself with all his names barring the titles. To go by the western system and only use the last name is often incorrect.

Here are some examples:

Mian Abdul Latif — Mian is the caste name. Pakistanis will politely address him with Mian Sahib. He will introduce himself as Abdul Latif. Friends will call him Latif and the foreigner may best call him Mr Latif.

Choudhry Abdul Latif — Choudhry shows that he is a landholding person or comes from such a family and is definitely from the provinces of Punjab or Sindh. Again, Choudhry Sahib holds traditional respect and courtesy. Often, he uses Choudhry at the end of the name. The visitor may call him Mr Choudhry, but since there are thousands of them it might lead to confusion.

Ghulam Hussein — Lower staff and household servants are normally called by their first names, without the title Sahib. But here, to call the man Ghulam would be wrong as the word means slave. The name makes sense only when used in conjunction with the other name: Ghulam Hussein, Slave of Hussein, which the father gave to the son out of reverence for the Muslim martyr Hussein.

Abdul Latif Janjua — Here, Janjua is the clan name and follows the personal name. He may be called Mr Janjua or Mr Latif or, very formally, Mr Abdul Latif.

Zia-ud-Din — Mr Din would be wrong as Din means Divine Law. In toto, the name means the Light of the Divine Law, and the person with that name should therefore be called either Mr Zia or

Mr Zia-ud-Din.

In the North West Frontier Province and in Baluchistan, the most common titulation is Khan which establishes the man as a Pathan. Mr Khan is widely used in urban society. It is different when Pakistanis call the man Khan Sahib. Then, it is a mixture of respect, seniority and leadership in a tribal context. Mohammed Jamal Khan may be the full name. You never use the word Mohammed when addressing people. Either Jamal or Mr Jamal or, formally, Mr Khan or Mr Jamal Khan.

When a person has the name Juma Khan or Tikka Khan he cannot just be called Juma or Tikka, because Juma means Friday and Tikka means meat on a skewer! Often, Pathans also use the name of their tribe as part of the name: Amjad Javed Khalil. Khalil is the tribe, and the person may be addressed as Mr Khalil. That's easy. After that, there is the problem of Amjad and Javed: each is a fully fledged personal name needing no additions. Usually, the first name is then used: Amjad, or Mr Amjad, though no harm is done by calling him Mr Amjad Javed. And, since he is called Khalil, which is a Pathan tribe, he may still be addressed as Khan Sahib which does him great honour.

The simplest way out of the maze is to ask the person by which name he is called or wants to be called, and the foreigner will very quickly learn how to go about names.

Lower staff speak about and address their superiors by their designation plus the word Sahib: Director Sahib, Engineer Sahib, Doctor Sahib and so on.

Lastly we come to women. The words Mrs or Miss are commonly used now, plus the husband's name which is beginning to become the family name. Begum is the Urdu equivalent of Mrs, to be followed by the husband's name; by implication, it comes much closer to the word madam. Servants call the mistress of the house Begum Sahib (Sahiba). When referring to someone's wife, he respectfully says Mr Latif's Begum. To write on the envelope of an invitation Begum Latif instead of Mrs Latif makes a world of difference.

In circles of less social sophistication, a woman is called by her personal name followed by the word Bibi (dear woman). So you have Rana Bibi and Surreya Bibi, all through the hundreds of very beautiful sounding names. A young woman or a girl whose name is not known may be called just Bibi.

A word of advice: When you look for Amjad Javed Khalil in the telephone directory, look it up under A, J *and* K before you give up!

Within the family, names are even more confusing to the foreigner. When you visit a friend's home, you may notice that the lady of the house is called khala or baji or p'huppi by the different members of the family. All these names are appellations that establish the relationship she has with the others.

The society of the Sub-continent has always lived in close interdependence of all relatives, if not always in the joint family system, and therefore has come up with a unique system of address. When someone calls a woman p'huppi, he or she says sister of our father. This pinpoints the relationship of each to the other in a remarkably swift and accurate way. To call people, particularly elders, by their names is considered improper in this status conscious society that expects verbal expressions of respect; its non-application leaves room to many interpretations as to what the defaulter might have meant to express.

A woman would thus be addressed in the following ways by the following persons:

apa (or baji)	by her younger sisters and brothers
khála	by her sisters' children
mami (or momani)	by the children of her husband's sisters
ch'háchi	by the children of her husband's younger brothers
tá'i	by the children of her husband's elder brothers

p'húppi	by the children of her brother
báhu	by her parents-in-law
náni	by the children of her daughters
dádi	by the children of her sons
bhábi	by the sisters- and brothers-in-law
patíji	by her aunts and uncles
sas	by her daughter-in-law
nànd	by her brother's wife
sali	by the husband of her sister

There are terms like hamzulf (the husband of my wife's sister) which are not used as forms of address, but to establish the degree of relationship when you talk about them. These people whose relationship with you is not so immediate will be addressed as bhá'iján (dear brother) and baji (dear sister). A person may call the wife of his very dear friend bhabi (sister-in-law), meaning thereby that she can trust him and lay claim to his help as if he were her real brother-in-law.

There are the same number or more, terms for male relatives. But better try to find your way through this labyrinth before looking at more.

The suffix 'ji' (for respect) and 'jan' (for love) at the end of the relationship-term lends a charming tone of respect and endearment to the address: Mamaji and Amajan are frequently heard. Well integrated women servants also call the mistress of the house baji.

Once a young man told me that he had 72 brothers. I was aghast and so embarrassed I could not even ask how many mothers were involved in this. After a few visits to his home it dawned on me that the 72 were all cousins, barring a few, 6 or 7, real brothers. The relationship among first cousins is mostly so close that they call each other, and in all daily matters, regard each other as brothers. The situation changes over matters like inheritance. Then they differentiate between sag'he b'hai (real brother) and just b'ha'i (cousin-brother). They will use this term, 'my cousin-brother', when they translate it for you into English.

THE SOCIAL GROUPS AND FORMS OF ADDRESS

The newcomer will very quickly see that society in Pakistan is split into different groups. Some are of a religious and sectarian nature; these, the visitor may ignore in the context of his social relationship with them. Many are of caste and tribal affiliation; these, too, can remain outside the foreigner's concern. Very many are of economic nature — and here we come very close to the type of groups the outsider will have to deal with in his daily life: the class system which dictates behaviour, lifestyle expectations, profession, marriages and careers. This is a legacy of the centuries' old interaction with Hindu society of the united India days and does hardly exist in other Muslim states as Islam is egalitarian.

Classes

The lowest class are the sweepers. In cities, they live in ghetto-like settlements consisting of mud huts. The sweeper comes to your home daily for floor cleaning; in less developed areas, he will also empty the pot of the commode — the toilet system that the British colonists preferred before flush toilets came to the country. He or she will not touch anything except furniture and nobody touches him unless he is ill. He does not expect it either. When he is thirsty, he will drink (hopefully chilled) water from an old tin.

The sweepers are mostly Christians. On Christmas night, they go through the streets singing carols. They are given monetary gifts by their various masters which should make them happy on this one great day of the year. If you do not want to be disturbed in the middle of the night you give him or her your Christmas gift the morning before Christmas. Nobody will then come near your house. Some masters like to invite them into the hall to sing, and treat them to cookies and sweets.

Your cook, gardener, *chowkidar* (watchman), driver (both at home and in your office) and the messenger boy all stand on the next rung up the social ladder. You address them all by their personal name (Yusuf Masih means Joseph the Christian and you call him Yusuf) without the Mr or Mrs.

In recent years, due to mass migration to oil-rich countries, skilled labour has become a rare commodity. Artisans are normally quite well off, though the trend still persists to go home and spend the earnings of two weeks' labour. If you need a workman, get him first on a trial basis; anyone who has ever felled a tree calls himself a carpenter.

If you call a dignified, older or efficient workman with the English appellation Mr, it often promotes the quality of work. Locally such persons would be called 'Mistry Sahib' (Mr Artisan).

In most households the workman gets a cup of tea and biscuits during the morning and in the afternoon. Do not leave him alone in a room where your possessions are lying about temptingly.

At the skilled, professional level, the class system is beginning to break down. People with modern professions like nurses, office assistants, secretaries, technicians, are persons you shake hands with and invite to a cup of tea with you. You always use Mr, Mrs or Miss when addressing them. They may refuse a tip or reward for a job well done or for an extra errand, but they do need it. Conceal it as a gift for the child or a cloth length for the wife, and always see them to the door. You are the master, but here you may smile.

There are some Christians who are professionals: teachers, doctors, lawyers and the like. They hold social status equal to Muslims in these professional lines. They prefer to speak English and often the women wear western dress. In many ways, they identify with the British. While they can rise professionally and socially, there is no such thing as a Christian Choudry or Khan.

Members of the modern urban society behave quite like their counterparts in all other countries. People like to be introduced by name and title, even if it is one of a private welfare organisation: 'Mrs Akbar, she is the General Secretary of our teachers' "Sunshine

Committee".' If you (a man) visit middle class homes in small towns or old parts of the city, be ready to eat the meal that is specially cooked for you, all alone or at best, together with the master of the house; women often eat after him anyway.

INVITATIONS AND SOCIAL ETIQUETTE

The country offers the most exciting entertainment when it comes to outings into nature, history, archaeology, palaeontology and so on. But when it comes to entertainment in the cities, there is very little choice; you mostly depend on your own resources or on friends. Therefore, friends meet frequently and guests are invited regularly. Sometimes, this means that a person has two or three dinner invitations for the same evening. He will then attend perhaps two of them for one or two hours each.

In smaller towns it is still customary to 'drop in', to visit neighbours and friends at the end of an evening stroll or drive. This visiting is mostly very rewarding, as it is totally informal. You may sip a cup of tea together and discuss what you like.

Punctuality

Pakistani parties are often somewhat stiff and follow a fixed pattern. Guests arrive about 10 minutes to one hour late for a private dinner. Among certain social groups particularly in Karachi, a party may start 3 hours late. You need to mind read your host to make sure that you don't arrive at a time when the caterers are just unloading the dining tables! A hostess should plan parties for nights when there is no English film programme on TV, or for a time when a popular TV programme is over. Guests will not consider they have any commitment to the host but will only pursue their own maximum pleasure, which may mean three functions per night!

National leaders have set a very bad example on punctuality. Ministers and other functionaries of the state, more often than not, come about one hour or more late to an inauguration, speech, dinner or show, and are trendsetters for a society that loves to demonstrate wealth and power in public. Don't believe for a minute that the other guests are upset over the late arrival of the chief guest. Where you would leave after a wait of 30 minutes, people here accept the situation — and imitate it!

The amazing duplicity is that when a foreigner invites Pakistanis for 8 p.m., they arrive almost on the dot! And when they, in turn expect foreigners for dinner, they know that they had better be ready at 8 o'clock sharp!

We would recommend arriving late at a wedding. Unless you are a member of one of the bridal couple's families or close enough to them to share in the hullabaloo, it is better to arrive at least one hour late; that will reduce your sitting ordeal of 4-6 hours by at least 60 minutes. And that goes on not for one, but two or three days or more. A wedding reception in a hotel hardly lasts longer than three hours. But if you attend such a ceremony in a village you must be prepared to give it the whole day. Therefore, it's wise to arrive at about 1 p.m. when lunch will be served.

Normally, you are invited to a party by a printed card. For a reception, do not rely totally on the 'RSVP' or 'Regrets only'; invitees may not regret and not show up or keep silent and then turn up. Generally, the number of guests evens out.

On occasions for which you receive a formal invitation, men will mostly come in a tie, or in shalwar kamis, the baggy trousers with the shirt over it. For this outfit, you need a smart waistcoat. When the invitation card says 'Dress formal', you had better don your dark suit. For formal invitations, as in the west, women should wear a formal dress, not necessarily full length but not tight fitting. A popular and elegant choice is to wear a sari — it takes practice to put one on and wear it, but is well worth the effort.

Weddings are the occasions when women may indulge in their finest and most expensive wear, with plenty of jewellery, extravagant hairstyles and sophisticated make-up. The finery and display are unbelievable and can never be matched — the western mind simply can't work that way! Rest assured that the other women inspect you as closely (and always benevolently) as they scrutinize each other — not so benevolently — and can recount after a month what every woman wore that evening!

Gifts

The western tradition of bringing small guest gifts has only recently made its entry here, and only at small private gatherings in cities. To express gratitude to your host, you may bring flowers (from your garden perhaps), a cake, a box of sweetmeats, dates or dried fruit . But if you go to spend a weekend with friends, you take a large basket with fruits or dried fruit, a piece of embroidery, a table cloth or such a present. Before you leave after a happy weekend there, make sure the servants of the house participate in your happiness in the form of a good tip.

Pakistanis are always happy when a foreigner attends a family wedding. Your 'Mubarak' (congratulations) to the families of the bride and groom and your admiration of the bride and the wedding arrangements and meal will long be remembered. Casual wedding guests are not expected to bring a gift; your presence is considered an honour for the whole family. But if you wish, you may take a gift: anything from table cloths, towels, decorative ornaments to handbags, cosmetic sets or suit-pieces, you have endless choice. Hand your gift (with a card on it) to the lady who receives you or ask her to whom you should give it. Pakistanis often give cash gifts in an envelope; this is not expected of foreigners but again if you wish, you may do this.

The Dinner Party

All types of party culminate in a meal. After that, you may leave immediately if you wish to. The meal comes at the earliest at 10 p.m. If alcohol is served, don't try your meal on male guests before

11 p.m. or you will have to warm it up again. Unless a Pakistani guest asks for it, it is better not to offer him an alcoholic drink. The experienced expatriate host may ask him: 'Do you want a tea or coffee or coke or something else?' In a small family gathering the hosts, knowing that in the west people eat their dinner early, might serve the food at 9 p.m., but don't rely on it and eat a biscuit before leaving home. It will be esteemed very highly if, as host, you send a plate of the meal (or tea and biscuits in the evening) to the driver of your guest who will eat it in the car, verandah or in the kitchen.

Remember that a Pakistani does not consider dinner as dinner if he does not get a hot meal. Cold meats, salads and dips are nice extras but that alone will not give him the feeling of having eaten his dinner. The Pakistani guest will feel well attended and consider your hospitality gracious if you ask him once or twice to have another helping —you may even put a choice piece of chicken on his plate over his mild protest. Be sure you discern between a genuine offer and unwanted insistance. The Pakistani is a hearty eater and does not require endless repetitions of formality.

A Pakistani treats a table napkin as a piece of formality. Eating manners are clean and, if they eat the rice or roti and curry with their hands, they will definitely be washed after the meal. Therefore, many families have a small wash basin right in their dining room. In rural environments some servants will pass by the eaters with a jar of warm water, soap and a towel. At weddings the arrangements for washing hands occupy a corner or side of the eating tent or hall.

A Pakistani handles fork and knife naturally only if he has had enough contact with foreigners. Tradition-conscious people may cut the roast on their plates with either fork, knife or spoon and then use the spoon for eating. Don't expect conformity in eating manners. Also, burping is a traditional expression of satisfaction which the host should hear. The more western and modern the environment, the less burps you will hear.

You must have toothpicks on the table as after the meal most

Pakistanis will clean their teeth; if they don't have water and basin around, they will reach for the toothpick. The results of the dental explorations are often lined up on the rim of the plate.

At meals, water is drunk. For treats, cola and other bottled drinks have started appearing on the dinner party table.

Mostly, men and women sit in different groups. Sitting in different rooms has become very rare except in rural landlord environments and with Pathans. Wherever the two sexes mix casually it would, however, be considered improper for a man to seat himself on a sofa where a Pakistani lady is already sitting.

If something drops from your handbag, do not expect anyone to pick it up for you. The gentlemen around you might make the odd gesture but not really mean it (unless one among them is western educated), which may result in an embarrassing situation. Servants will act only reluctantly or when told. To bend thus for others is a show of servility and the ground level is unclean, and the class conscious Pakistani shrinks from it.

Toilets

The toilets of the world are many and varied, and Pakistan has a variety of them. It is a strict rule that the cleaning after defecation must be done with the left hand. No food is to be touched with this hand. It is unclean. There is an Islamic law that demands that for the offence of serious theft, one hand, by tradition the right hand, is cut off. It is an even more serious sentence than at first appears. Since tradition prohibits the touching of food with the left hand, the punishment is equal to a death sentence — from starvation; or the offender may eat but live a life in hiding.

In the old city houses, two to three storeys high, there are small areas, on the flat roof where the families sleep in summer. Hidden behind a brick enclosure there are the family toilets: the narrow bricked well goes right down to the ground level — the sewer. It is difficult for flies to get that low and for smells to get that high.

Town and village dwellers are conscious of the fact that the old systems are a problem for the foreign guest. You may, therefore, be taken to a store-room and see a four-legged stool. The wooden top of the stool is not a seat but a lid. Open it, and you find the real seat under it with a hole cut out in the middle from which a small bucket hangs down. It is an invention of the British Empire's colonial days and is still in use, also in remote hill stations and far flung holiday resorts. In such far flung hotels, a sweeper is constantly in attendance. Just open the back door that every such bathroom has and the bucket will again be clean for use within a few minutes.

Modern city houses have the latest flush systems, one with every bedroom. But often, you do not find toilet paper. People widely observe the Islamic system of washing after defecation, so instead, you find next to the toilet the famous *lota*, a round-bellied plastic (or even brass and copper) mug with a long spout. You find the lota standing among the boxes and quiltrolls, babies and chickens at long-distant bus-stops and on railway stations. A modern version of it is the toilet shower, a most hygenic invention indeed.

If you have guests from a town or older city house, do not be surprised to find your toilet seat muddied, dirty or trampled afterwards. For conservative Muslims it is unthinkable to sit bare-bottomed on the same seat on which others sat likewise before him. So he will squat on your toilet! In many houses and in public toilets you find the pedestal flush toilet which is more hygenic than the seat toilet — though a problem for foreigners who have not learnt to squat.

Making Friends

The Pakistanis are a sociable people; if you ask for the way, you will sooner be invited to tea than shown the direction. But urban living has undermined the old concepts of hospitality. In the city it is easy to get into social conversation but not any more easy to get to know people well. To be taken to a Pakistani home other than through a

TICKETS

Pakistanis will always take a lota with them on a long journey.

formal invitation is usually a sign that the person is extending you his hand in friendship.

The Meaning of a Friend

The word 'friend' is something of greatest significance in Pakistan. A person has many friends, because he needs them. The traditional

59

feudal and bureaucratic systems have made it imperative for a man to have friends in the health, education, police, finance, legal, electricity and other such life supporting departments — or he is a loser. Only through friends are jobs done, applications moved, admissions granted or the line repaired. Otherwise, one simply trails at the end of the hundreds of cases that will be dealt with 'in the near future'.

Persons in positions of influence know what they owe their friends. Being a friend is a serious business, and never a one-sided one. The other party is definitely expected to make returns when the need arises and in accordance with his own resources. Do not think that friendships here are of utilitarian nature from the start. They generally follow the ideal of friendship and they mostly last a lifetime. Even sitting with another person on the same school bench is a bond that normally lasts for life.

With a foreigner, there are some other motives that prompt a person to establish a friendship. Often, a Pakistani feels he can talk freely with a foreign friend and be his natural self unchecked by the constraints of status or tradition. People in towns and villages moreover feel it an honour to be a friend to a foreigner; all they ask for is cultural recognition. It is said that a Pathan is 'either a good friend or a bad enemy'. He will go to great lengths to prove worthy of your friendship. And should a Pathan give you a ring of friendship, it is a very serious matter. Even if you meet him again after 20 years, be prepared to go out of your way to fulfil his wishes, or do not accept the ring.

People depend on each other for their socio-cultural needs much more than in the West. The casual chatty hour after sunset is often the climax of the day and goes a long way in establishing lifelong friendships. A man intensely relates his life to other men. In fact, when a man lives alone by choice or by force of circumstances it disturbs a Pakistani friend's mind. It is not natural and he will try to keep him company as often as he can. And a foreigner who also sees the interhuman relationship as a very important aspect of life and equally desires his company is naturally included.

WOMEN IN PAKISTAN

Burquah and Purdah

The full length cover that many women wear when they go out of the house is called burquah. There are two types: one of black, silky material which consists of a long sleeved coat or cloak. From the crown of the head, a separate, wide cloth falls over the back and shoulders. It is held on the head by a string tied under the chin, like a huge, black scarf. At the hairline in front, three thin black veil-pieces are stitched into this headcloth to cover the face. When the woman scrutinizes a piece of material in the shop, she will throw them back over the head or arrange them in such a way that, from ear to ear, they cover her face leaving the eyes free. When she comes out on the street, she will drop one, two or all the three veils over her face. Now, she sees the world around her through a local type of 'dark glasses'. When she sits in a car or on a tonga or bus, she mostly keeps just one of the veils down, the other two are thrown back over the head.

This is the fashionable kind of burquah worn mostly by middle and lower middle class women in cities and towns. Some of the girls in colleges and universities also use it; they come from this environment and do what their parents order them to do.

Then, there is the 'shuttlecock' burquah: a white thick cotton material tightly fitted over the head. From the border of this cap falls an enormous mass of white cotton cloth in tight plaits right down to the heels — when the wind blows it up, it looks like a shuttlecock! Over the eyes, a square piece is cut out and replaced by a thick net of criss-cross strings that leaves out little squares through which the woman can see her immediate surroundings. The women behind this type of burquah mostly come from small towns or villages. On the other hand, rural women in their own environments do not wear the burquah — they would not be able to do the hard work in the house and field that they are required to do. City women take off the burquah when they reach their offices and arrange the thin fine veil, the dupatta, beautifully over their heads, shoulders or around the neck — each way signifies a certain stage of emancipation.

Sometimes, girls who come from liberal homes don the burquah after marriage if the husband so rules, but mostly it's the other way around. In small towns, in lower middle class environments you see more of the burquah than in modern urban enviroments.

When a woman wears the burquah, avoids going out, and never goes out unaccompanied, when she does not attend mixed parties or receive male guests, this is called purdah, the system of living behind the veil. The woman then 'observes purdah'.

A woman observing purdah will avoid going to the bazaar and does it only if no child or male family member is around. Islam demands that women be decently dressed and cover their arms up to the wrist. There is nothing in the Koran that orders them to cover their faces.

The educated lady of the city has discarded the burquah. She may keep one in the closet for a journey to far flung areas or when visiting her relatives in the village. This educated urban woman of the affluent society lives out her femininity through buying and wearing plenty of expensive clothes, frequent visits to the hairdresser, a display of jewellery, rich use of perfumes, sophisticated make-up, and by attending many parties and inviting guests frequently to prove her talents as a gracious hostess. Women other than these, prefer to keep their hair in the classical style of the Sub-continent: straight back and worked into a thick, long plait.

Girls and Schools

In cities, almost all girls attend school; in villages, the percentage of school-going girls is below 10 per cent; in tribal areas, below 5 per

Four typical styles of Pakistani women's head dress: the 'shuttlecock' burquah-clad style of town or village; the educated yet traditional family woman; the modern urban socialite who dares to cut her hair short; and the urban middle class traditionally modest style.

63

cent. Girls are highly talented. They often come out ahead of boys in the final school examinations. At secondary level, the number of girls drops sharply. Many parents think it is easier to find a husband if their daughter displays her modesty by wearing a burquah. Then, to let her unfold her personality through greater knowledge can only lead to trouble.

Women at Work

Some typically female professions such as teaching and nursing are open to women without major criticism from orthodox circles. But women fight a permanent battle, mostly at home against fathers, uncles and particularly brothers, to allow them to adopt a professional career. Often, the family will compromise and allow the girl to teach in a kindergarten or primary school until a husband is found. It is perhaps increasing economic pressure that brings more and more women into offices, banks, industry, and even on the TV screen and into hotel and airline service. Many religious minded families regard such girls as immoral as they work side by side with men. This reputation, of course, does them no good when it comes to finding a husband. Women observing purdah have to buy tickets for three bus seats for long travel so that no man may sit next to them on the bench.

The educated and emancipated lady of the cities sometimes overacts in her endeavour to be considered as modern as a western woman. It is an expression of her keenness to dissociate herself from the orthodox thinking on women. Women's organisations and the WAF, the Women's Action Forum, are trying to give women financial, material and moral support in their struggle to be considered equal human beings with men.

Foreign Women and Dress

I have seen foreign women arrive here in shorts and strapless vests. Such dress does no good to the image of western women in the east!

Women on public transport: since the two-seater women's section of this mini bus is full, the women wait patiently for the next and the next... Squatting comes naturally to them and makes waiting more comfortable.

This normally either outrages religious feelings, causes embarrassment and forces many to look away; or else it invites trouble.

There is one simple rule for dress: keep your body, legs and forearms covered. It is better to buy a loose fitting dress than a tight fitting one. In urban society, a normal knee-length dress will hardly be noticed; but if you want to avoid or reduce stares in the bazaar, jeans, trousers, a long dress or Pakistani dress are the answers — and beautiful options.

The Pakistani dress is comfortable and suitable in all weathers: in winter, it is just right for the mild chill in the air while in summer, it absorbs sweat. The kamis (shirt) can be bought ready-made or tailored in any fashion or style. The most suitable one is always a cotton or cotton mix material; in summer, try lawn, a very fine cotton cloth. Pakistani women consume unimaginable lengths of cloth and you will find it a problem to make your choice from the huge varieties of colours and prints in the endless cloth bazaars. It seems to be the major occupation of urban women to buy cloth — the shops are never less than crowded.

If you wear jeans or trousers you might like to match them with a blouse or sweater that falls loosely over the hips to the thighs. You can have it tailored here and, with a stylish belt, turn it into an elegant evening outfit. Generally, you can get your dresses stitched by tailors in the bazaar or by 'verandah-tailors' whom you hire for a week or a month at home. What with the variety of beautiful cotton prints and fine, inexpensive silks, many foreign women have their wardrobes made here to last them for the next ten years!

Nowadays, more and more boutiques are opening up that have ready made garments, sometimes including western dresses. Some women find it easier to buy there than go through the hassle of instructing a tailor day in day out, trying again and again — and not too infrequently, ending up with a total misfit! While tailors are good at design, they can cut much better when they are given a ready made dress to copy.

To all visiting women, the sari, the classical dress of the Sub-continent, is a great attraction. And there is hardly a dress that can beat the sari in elegance.

Getting Ready

Pakistani women take great trouble over their appearance even when it just means going to the bazaar or to the movies. It is always an occasion! The suit is carefully chosen, ironed and worn after a bath. The make-up takes ages, but women are experts at it!

Most Pakistani women are naturally beautiful, but on two counts, even less attractive women will always fascinate a foreigner: the very large, clear, black eyes under thick long eyelashes emphasised with antimony; and the thick, black, dense and very long hair. Apart from modern city ladies, Pakistani women wear their hair in the classical style, straight back and tied into a plait that swings around the hips.

It is hard to understand for a westerner that, when grace, beauty, dress, jewellery, hair and make-up render a picture of vibrant beauty — down comes the burquah, so that the lady can walk like a black shroud through the streets.

TOPICS OF CONVERSATION

Small Talk

The world over women talk about their daily concerns: children, illness, servants, income, prices, cloth, cooking or the whims of their husbands. Barring a few nuances it is quite the same everywhere.

It is only natural that women must find an object on which they can unload and express their personalities. Very often, it is the daughter-in-law, servants, young children, or a friend. I have often been amazed at the bargaining skills Pakistani women friends have boasted of, and when I have asked shopkeepers for a similar price, I have often been laughed at. The women had understated the actual price they had paid in order to highlight their achievement before other women.

A mixture of exaggeration and each woman's self-perception applies equally well to shopping skills as to talk of husbands. Either they are luckier than anybody else or the most wretched of all maltreated wives! Women also speak astoundingly freely to one another about their intimate sex experiences.

And Men?

Among men, office achievements, progress and treachery are all regular topics of conversation; so is politics, often discussed heatedly. A display of wealth, such as a new car, will lead to silent speculation on the owner's wealth, income and connections in industry and government. Women and religion are touchy subjects best avoided by foreigners: you can mention your wife, but without any details of intimacy and you should not joke about women.

Among very close friends, Pakistanis will joke in the vernacular — not even in Urdu — and will also discuss any problems of illness or education concerns within their families.

Women in the Family

The relationship between the husband and wife in public is very formal. In lower middle class circles, he will always walk in front with his sons, and the wife follows after them with the daughters. When the husband comes from abroad after a prolonged absence, his welcome at the airport consists of a shy 'salam' with eyes cast down; at best, at the most modern, a brief hug. The Pakistani on-looker feels embarrassed when a western couple meets in a public place, even at the airport, with a western-style embrace and kiss.

Mostly, husband and wife address each other with the formal 'ap'. Only very modern couples speak about and address each other by their names. In most families, the husband will be referred to as 'father of Aslam' by his wife, and the wife as 'mother of Aslam' by the husband. When addressed, no name is used, or a surrogate title. In front of servants, husband and wife refer to each other as 'Sahib' and 'Begumsahib'. The traditional Pakistani wife keeps her dupatta on her head in the presence of her husband.

In an average family the woman is as much the centre of the household as in most other countries. She plays her traditional role: keeps the house in order, the clothes washed and in good repair; she prepares the meals and brings up her children, teaches them and watches over their health. It's mostly the wife who looks after the social interests of the family members. She decides what is to be purchased. In case of expensive items, she would consult with her husband or leave the decision to him. Fathers mostly decide what the son should study and, possibly, where he should work later on, though in some families, the choice is left to the sons. Both parents decide to whom their grown up children should be married.

While doing her work, a woman may drop the cumbersome

dupatta, the thin veil. The moment a man or an elder enters the room, she will hastily pick it up and drape it over her head or over her shoulders at least. When the woman observes very strict purdah, the husband has to arrange all the shopping and the woman will cook according to his purchases.

Pakistani women are generally weak at organising, with a day's activities often unplanned and full of diversions. But time is not money here and the woman draws out her occupations to keep herself busy. Still, she often complains of the emptiness of a life that does not allow her to fulfil her entire personality.

In case of an unmarried girl, the brother has a great say in her doings, and it's not uncommon for a brother to stop his sister from studying because of co-education in universities. Her schooling then ends behind the *char divari*, the four walls to which tradition-alists insist women must limit their activities.

— Chapter Five —

FAMILY LIFE

On first impression the streets in Pakistan are devoid of beauty.
There are no fine buildings and housefronts, there is no art in the
decor of the shopwindow displays, no theatre, no lightness in the
air, no announcements of cultural entertainment... Instead, there are
walls: high, ugly, old, mighty, dirty, broken and artistic. And all life
in Pakistan takes place behind these walls.

In the slow lifestyles of the Sub-continent, drama has only come
up recently. There are rudimentary efforts by theatre groups, but
hardly any public theatre halls exist. The state-controlled television
and the private film industry adopted and developed drama in two

diverse directions. Films are largely vulgar, melodramatic and artificial. If you are ready to invest three solid hours you will be rewarded with a lot of shooting, hip swinging, car racing and also the hero chasing the heroine till she plucks a flower and, while tears run down her full cheeks under a full moon, she sings a heartthrobbing song. Television has taken a different course. The dramas depict the struggle of women, criticise social behaviour and educate the mostly illiterate masses. Even though you won't understand a single word, seeing a drama on television is a worthwhile study of the Pakistani way of life, moods and customs.

The classical music of the Sub-continent dates back to the early Middle Ages. It is a system of highest sophistication and requires a separate book to explain the basics. In most cases the ear that is not used to this type of music takes quite some time to be able to appreciate it.

Again, concerts are largely private affairs. It is rare that an organisation arranges a classical music programme in a hotel hall or auditorium of a college or company. The big cities have music societies that hold regular recitals. To attend, you need to be a member and need to know the right people to get in. Young beat-groups organise 'shows' on western lines — but all male of course. Fashion shows are run by boutiques, mostly in hotels. You need to find out where to buy a ticket. Organisers of exhibitions have lists of art lovers whom they invite.

You can be a member of a foreign cultural association or of the Asian Study Group, a private organisation run by foreigners that arranges excellent talks, outings and demonstrations on all aspects of Pakistani and Asian life.

Members, lists, private shows... the new arrival needs the help of an experienced expatriate to get to the right address and cultural circle of interest.

But the actual Pakistani culture is basically not a performing or exhibiting one, but lives itself out in the personal behaviour and

71

social relationships. And that happens behind house or coutyard walls. When you pass through the rather unseemly outer boundary wall, you will be surprised to find behind it a lush garden and a traditional or modern house. The Islamic lifestyle traditionally does not demonstrate its inherent value and culture to the public eye. The dividing line is the wall: outside it, is the general public; you have nothing to do with that. Inside the wall is where you live and express yourself. It is a feudal attitude which was enhanced through the system of purdah.

To experience Pakistani life and culture, you need to penetrate the wall.

Hospitality

One of the foremost cultural traits of the Pakistani who is conscious of his cultural tradition is hospitality. It is therefore not unusual to be invited to the homes of Pakistani friends. A well-to-do Pakistani has a large sitting room in his home for guests. In the West, this would often constitute the entire living area. Meanwhile he and his family live in a lounge that is the central hall to which all doors lead, or on the stair landing, often furnished with odd, old chairs, a hard divan, occasionally a rug and the television set.

Since the sitting room for guests is not used daily, it sometimes has a museum-like atmosphere which is enhanced by the stiffness of the furniture arrangement. Only a few homes have preserved the charm of low sitting on cushions and fine rugs with small tea tables at the side. Although the low sitting can often be uncomfortable for the expatriate, it can be easier if the ladies wear Pakistani dress or trousers. Most homes now have changed to sitting on high chairs; generally you find the expensive sofa sets in a formal square arrangement that does not allow a relaxed style of entertainment. This style of hospitality is a remnant of earlier times when ritual dominated a guest's visit. As only the headman could then afford to entertain guests outside a family gathering, his style and display of splendour was perpetuated and copied. Even an enemy, should he set foot in your tent, had to be honoured as a guest. But let him set one foot out of it and he was no longer safe. The ceremony of a guest-gift, a guest-feast, a guest-cultural-display is still observed in small towns and villages and in the homes of clans and tribes.

Next, in a modern sitting room you notice a hotch potch of disparate ornaments: perhaps an array of expensive Bohemian crystal placed on plastic mats, a Japanese coffee pot in modern-baroque style which plays music when you lift it, a giant synthetic cuckoo clock, a Venus of plaster of Paris and a picture of a Greek temple.

Clan Ties

Clan and family ties are — still — very close. Even if there is dissent among certain members of a family, they always include each other as statutory components of the group that cannot be split. The awareness of bonds, of roots, is very strong and gives people the sense of belonging, from which they receive their strength. No doubt, individuality is sometimes submerged at the cost of clan identity. It is more usual to identify a person through his father or grandfather rather than through the individual's merits. The family is like a guarantee that his blood is good in a moral sense too. Modern urban living is gradually changing this family concept.

THE JOINT FAMILY SYSTEM

How would you feel if your great-grandparents, your grandparents, your parents, your children, your grandchildren and perhaps their children lived with you under the same roof? This has been the pattern for centuries with all its advantages and curses. The juniors have to obey their seniors even if they themselves are over 50 years old and want to have their say or determine their own spending. The bread-earning members of the family are obliged to feed and clothe each member who does not earn. This is the crux of the family system — whether joint or not — and provides a kind of a pension for the seniors.

This explains the need to have sons and the agony when daughters are born. Sons provide for their parents till their death; daughters leave the house and, moreover, need dowries to be able to leave the house; to stay unmarried would mean life-long financial obligations on the father or brother, or maybe even on a brother-in-law.

Even if a son has settled with his family far away from home, he is sure to send his parents every month as much as he can save from his mostly very modest living expenses. When you see an old man of a remote and poor area sporting a transistor radio you can be sure that his son works in the Gulf. Pakistan's largest and most regular flow of foreign exchange comes from the remittances that its labour force working abroad is regularly sending home!

Apart from providing sustenance for the parents, the joint family system is also meant to keep the ageing people company. It is almost as important as the food. Elders are not to be left alone. There need not be ceaseless conversation, but the human nearness gives the seniors the sense of shelter and protection.

Imagine 20 people or so living under the same roof with you! Even if the roof is large, the strains on the individuals are great. Elders make full use of the juniors. The younger they are the more they have to be prepared to be called upon to serve them. There is a cup of tea due; the newspaper has to be found and the hair needs dyeing. A massage is required daily and a piece of lace is to be purchased. A letter needs to be written and is to be mailed. There was just a knock at the door and the right TV programme is to be turned on... Younger ones bow their heads before the elders, women drape the dupatta over their heads. Nobody speaks back on any issue. In situations where forgiveness is to be asked, the foot of the elder is to be touched as a sign of total submissiveness.

When an elder person stretches out his or her arms to you, do bend forward for the embrace during which you will receive his or her blessing. Let the gesture of selfless goodwill and affection enter you. It is a fine and, for the westerner, rare experience. Take the offered seat and accept happily the expressions of esteem that are due to a guest. Try a conversation of gestures. There will be a meal or, at least, tea. After that you may ask: 'Ejazet hai?' (May I beg leave?) When you go out you may feel sure that you have made some souls perfectly happy that day. Often, on visiting for the first time you will be given guest presents, mostly some pieces of cloth. You might like to take a similar gift for the eldest lady in the house — but in any case, enough toffees or biscuits for all the children.

The Daughter-in-Law

The greatest sufferer in a joint family system is invariably the daughter-in-law. Her main role is to serve her parents-in-law, even at the cost of serving her husband. Where the husband works away from his home town, his wife and children are often not allowed to live with him there because the mother-in-law needs them more. If there are unmarried daughters of the mother-in-law under the same roof they will see to it that their sister-in-law is kept busy.

Even if there is great harmony among all the members of the joint family under the same roof, there is little privacy or silence. Yet, there is no better system. Pakistanis look down upon the western institution of old age homes as something inhuman. It is unthinkable that the son should not keep his ageing parents with him.

However, hardly noticed and not discussed, in modern urban environments a trend has started for young couples to live away from the man's old parents, mostly on the insistance of the young wife. Also, in the developing industrial areas, living accommodation is scarce particularly since the birthrate is extremely high. In both situations, the old parents accept the necessity but lead quite a miserable life as they were never trained to live alone or to find other resources to lend colour to their fading lives.

The Guest

Expatriates are mostly very impressed by the status a guest has and the treatment and attention he receives with it. If you have a problem with a government office, shopkeeper, counter clerk or whatever, your wishes will be fulfilled, your problem solved and a facility provided for you — because you are a guest in the land. And this, in the presence of ten locals who have complained or applied ten weeks ago without success, and who will quietly submit to the preferential treatment you receive — because you are a guest. (Later, we shall talk about feelings against foreigners, see page 185.)

The expatriate should be aware that although there is no need to offer anything in return, his sentiments should be equally refined. He should express his gratitude to the person who helped him. Only low staff would try to take advantage of a foreigner for monetary gain. While the official's motive vis-à-vis the foreigner is his view that you, as a guest, must be offered hospitality, he would do the same thing for a friend or relative as an obligation. It is quite a system and is called 'safarish', preferential treatment. Whoever enjoys safarish is lucky, and everyone would make use of it if they could. Therefore nobody in the queue complains: he would do the same if he were so lucky.

The expatriate should present his case in polite language, not humbly nor patronizingly, but as among equals. He should not be loud or hurried, or abuse a person or thing that has been the cause of his problem. Be cool! A bit of flattery does no harm, humour is even better. The expatriate would spoil his case and preferential treatment should he, as a guest who enjoys special status, jump the queue or press into a room or behave loudly or blame others.

Politeness and a little distance from others certify you as a gentleman. Hospitality is not without class consciousness. No doors will open to the unkempt tourist whose style is not that of a gentleman.

In the Home

There are two types of guests: the ones sitting in sitting-rooms — also called drawing rooms — and the ones in the family lounges. The sitting room atmosphere is formal. The room is opened for guests who do not know the family well. All conversation is polite and cool. If you have come to discuss an urgent issue, it will go down better if first you talk for a while on other matters after having asked about the welfare of each family member — about the wife, of course, in terms of mother of so and so. If you are a newcomer to the home, you are expected to be very interested in the family. Therefore, you will be shown the family photos. Your language problems, if there are any, may now recede to the background in the face of stacks of albums, mostly of wedding occasions.

If your hostess observes purdah, the husband and wife visitors will be taken to different rooms: the host will entertain the husband in the drawing room and the hostess the wife in the family lounge, or, in modest or traditional living environs, in the bedroom.

The bedroom is generally the living room for the family. The traditional bed consists of a simple wooden frame on legs, over which strings are stretched criss-cross. This is cool in summer, as your back, when you lie, is equally exposed to air. Or, a thin mattress stuffed with cotton is spread out which is rolled back during the day. These beds, called *charpoi*, then become the chairs on which the family squats; babies are dressed and nursed there; vegetables peeled; for a meal, a tray is put on it in the middle. The charpoi is an all-time table-chair-sofa-floor-bed.

If your stay in the country is long and you mix with families frequently, learn to squat on the charpoi right from the start. (Foreigners, though, will always be given a chair to sit on.) The frame of the bed will otherwise stop your blood circulation from the back of your knees downwards or will tell on your spine! During the day, the bedroom is the women's social area.

DON'T REFUSE

Mostly, tea will be brought; in village surroundings, where a foreign guest is something very special and where the host will glean a lot of prestige among the villagers for having such a guest, roasted chickens or other birds will be served to go with the tea.

Do not refuse any of these. They are delicious anyway. You do the host honour by accepting and enjoying his culinary entertainment or even asking for a little more of this or that. Mostly, titbits are salty; if you really do not want to eat of it, ask 'Mirch hai?'(is there chilli in it?). If there is some, there will be ready understanding for your refusal. The only other acceptable refusal is that you have an upset stomach and can take only light tea — with the emphasis on 'light'. Mostly, the tea is very strong, and it is cooked with the leaves for a minute at least. If it's too bitter, ask for some hot water to dilute it. It often comes mixed with the milk — sometimes the tea is cooked in milk, which is delicious — and one can easily get used to it. It's often very sweet, so if you are asked to have tea and do not like it with sugar, say so. Tea with salt, however, is something for experts. That comes with practice.

MEN'S SOCIAL LIFE

Traditionally, men spend their free time with friends away from home. The foreigner is always amazed when he sees the local wayside tea-stalls: at all times of the day, they are full of men. They sip a simple bowl of black or green tea rather noisily. In the North West Frontier Province you get the real taste of green tea; it comes in a handleless small bowl which must have at least one crack and several metal brackets to hold the pieces together. The green tea gets its real flavour in these. It is said that if the tea-stall owner has run out of broken and bracketed tea bowls, he breaks some new ones, glues them together and fixes them with brackets — or his business will slacken.

At tea stalls throughout Pakistan, there they sit on charpois, and however diverse the people or opinions might be, there is one uniting factor: the *hookah*.The hookah is the hubble-bubble or waterpipe, the traditional means of smoking. There are some extremely fine specimens, mostly in brass. The cheap ones are made of clay. They look like very large vases with narrow necks. Some foreigners like to convert them into lamp-bases. Their wide bottoms contain water, and the narrow necks are plugged by small containers holding the tobacco, which is sometimes mixed with sugar. A long pipe emerges from it with a mouthpiece at the end . When you draw, the smoke passes through the water and leaves the nicotine behind. But it also leaves behind a ghastly smell in the room, like a full, wet ashtray. Foreigners are not urged to share in the experience and it is wiser not to try it. Too much TB has been passed on from this mouthpiece.

There the men sit and listen and talk and talk and listen, day-in, day-out. Everybody has time, the wage-labourer, the tiller of the

An old man smoking the hookah.

soil, the clerk, the landowner. They talk about the three Zs (*Z'r, zamin, zanana*, i.e. gold, land and women), and listen to the stories of *Alif Laila* (*The Arabian Nights*) and to the news from the stock exchange, while the colourful oriental street life happens before their eyes.

SINGLE WOMEN

For the single woman life is not so easy. Whatever men do is right, and if it's not right it is not talked about. Not so for women. Their life pattern is narrowly circumscribed. When a man does not marry, he is the happy — or lucky — bachelor; if a girl does not marry, she could not find a match, so there must be something wrong with her.

The number of single working girls or women who live by themselves can be counted on your fingers. Such women are thought to be of dubious character. If working in the same office with men is supposed to corrupt a woman's mind, how much more is living by herself! Therefore, the unmarried girl, working or not, lives with her parents or a female relative. It is quite a blessing that most people do have plenty of relatives all over the country. But, in the unmentioned undercurrents of co-existence of the 'poor unmarried niece' with her relatives there is mostly untold misery for the young or ageing single woman. But it is the only safe-haven she has in the male-dominated world around her.

THE FAMILY ROUND THE CLOCK

As for everybody in the world, getting up early for work is one of the most unpleasant experiences in a Pakistani's life. Whoever can afford to sleep longer will do so. Therefore, if you are one of those who have dealings with a higher official, don't be at his office before nine at the earliest. Getting up late and getting late to the office is part of the status symbol — I am the boss, you see, I come by my own time! And when there is a downpour in the morning, do not come at all unless the sun is out again.

So, the Pakistani sahib of the city, after he or his driver has taken his children to their various schools (the getting-up time of women is never discussed), gets to his office around nine. In Karachi, the only city with a sort of nightlife plus many rich people, office bosses take their seats around eleven. And shopkeepers, except those who sell foodstuffs, follow suit, so don't go shopping before eleven.

This is the time when the Begumsahib has had her bath, has ordered the servants what to clean and what to cook and sets off in her limousine to pick up a few friends for a shopping spree.

The officer in government service gets home between two and three in the afternoon. He collects his children from their schools and the family then sits down to lunch which is always late. The private company executive hardly gets back before six in the evening. After the second bath of the day and fresh clothes, the family will have tea together. Then comes the time to visit friends, to drop in; to shop for something together, or 'go for a coke'. Then, it's time to get ready for the party or reception. If there isn't one that evening, the television has to help out. The TV normally remains switched on for hours together. Even when guests drop in, the TV stays on... a quick glance to keep abreast with the happening of the serial... and the conversation lumbers along. Often, dinner is brought on the trolley to the 'TV lounge' so that the important feature is not missed. Servants, when they are free, also watch, squatting at the door to the kitchen. Nobody remembers what people did when there was no TV!

Dinner is normally late, around 9 p.m. Children, even very young ones, are put to bed late. They are often brought along to parties and shows and create a disturbance there. But nobody minds.

Children

Children are the treasured possessions of the parents, particularly boys, as they are their old-age insurance. The difference between boys and girls is a factor in their upbringing at a very young age. Many more girls die of illness or malnutrition than boys under the age of five. Together with a little girl's growth in strength and understanding grow her duties: she is hardly four when she runs errands and carries and comforts the latest baby.

A little boy, however, leaves the mother's or other relatives' lap only to be put to bed. He is pampered and soon spoilt and arrogant.

To slap a little boy even when he screams his head off is considered cruel. The child, it is argued, does not know better and must therefore be given everything he wants. There are some clever little boys who rule the whole family! Thus, sex-roles are driven home from infancy. In Punjabi, there are lullabys for boys, not for girls. More than double the number of boys attend school as compared to girls.

The ordinary child's life knows few joys. Although children are very beautiful with their large eyes, thick black hair and fine, regular features, they hardly laugh. They look at you with the seriousness of little monks. When the boy is about six years old, the father begins to take him along to the mosque, the bazaar, his friends, and as the child moves in the company of adults his serious face gets set.

There is child labour in Pakistan. The poor send their little ones to earn their daily bread as they have hardly anything to feed them on. The most common are the boys of about ten washing cars and assisting mechanics, or serving in small restaurants, while the girls of eight carry the babies of the well-to-do and do the simpler chores in the kitchen. The fingers of adults can never replace the nimble fingers of ten year old boys in the entire carpet industry!

Children who attend prep schools and study in English medium schools know all the famous English nursery rhymes. The television is making a laudable effort to produce and teach children Urdu songs and rhymes. The toy industry is in a rudimentary stage and struggling. Products have to be cheap and are often so shoddy that they break on slightest impact. Only few can afford even these — there are too many children who only know empty boxes, cigarette packets and strings to play with. An expatriate might think that a fine educational toy will make such a child very happy. But mostly, he and his parents do not know what to do with it. Also, there would be more admiration coming from peers when he has just the doll or plastic car that the neighbours have. Educated families feel the lack of quality toys and wherever possible, make up by heavy imports of expensive toys and electronic toy gadgets.

There is one rule that applies to all children whether rich or poor: obedience to elders. Children will not speak back or argue, they will follow instructions minutely, be of help and attend to guests — there are some ten year olds who are perfect hostesses and conversationalists — and execute all the orders of their elders. And 'elders' start with the elder brother and sister! It is often debated among children what has more advantages and less disadvantages, to be the eldest child or the youngest!

Schools have no real discipline problems. The teacher wields such authority over the students that he or she is revered throughout life.

Birthdays

While the illiterates in villages do not know the exact dates of birth of their children — 'Ashraf was born after the holy month of Ramadan!' — modern city dwellers celebrate their darlings' birthdays with a great fanfare. The kids are dressed in their best clothes. When they have handed over their birthday gift, they are entertained under fancy buntings, coloured lights and balloons, to puppet shows, rides on and dances by hired camels, varieties of cakes and other goodies and take-home gifts. Often, all class mates are invited plus the neighbourhood. Mothers who bring their children may stay on so that a large group of ladies forms a substantial aspect of the party. It is advisable to prepare for this as ladies love a rich high tea.

THE PATHANS

The highest walls in the country are those of the Pathans or Pakhtoons, the tribes living in the tribal areas or even in the settled districts. The large tribes like the Khattaks, Waziris, Afridis, Mahsoods, Mohmands, Shinwaris, Yusufzais, etc, each numbering many tens of thousands, inhabit certain well defined areas: the Khattaks the land between Kohat, Bannu and the Indus in the west of the North

West Frontier Province. The Yusufzais are settled in the beautiful Swat valley and adjoining mountains in the north of the province. Within each tribe, there are large groups or sub-tribes. These, then, fall into large families who live together in a *killa*, the fortlike abode of some hundreds of family-members.

The Killa

The tribal belt is mountainous and barren. You approach a killa on a path the sand of which engulfs your car. Ahead, a square yellow mud-structure comes into view: the killa of your friend, who has invited you to his home for the day.

The killa is on average 100 metres square. The walls are at least 6 metres high. At certain intervals you see lookouts on the top of the walls — mostly unmanned now. The gate that opens to let you in is at least 4 metres high. Your dusty journey ends behind these 1 or 2 metre thick walls in a wide courtyard. Tribal elders will rush to greet you. You will be taken to the guestroom, the largest and best furnished room in the whole killa, of course. Sometimes, you will find a one hundred-year old Afghan carpet lying there. Then, usually, you find group photos of the tribal elders' school or college days, or of visits of dignitaries in the past on the mantlepiece.

Young boys run in and out bringing hot water and towels to freshen up your face from the dusty trip, cardamom-spiced green tea (nobody can prepare green tea as the Pathans do), and fruit. Conversation is always slow and never light. From the parapet you have an imposing view of the ruggedness and hostility of their mountain world and you begin to understand the Pathan character. They will explain to you (there are always some who speak English) who are friends and foes in the other killas in the valley; their warfare against so many enemies, their deeds of chivalry.

The Meal

You will soon find lunch served on the large table. And there is

Tribal elders awaiting a guest of honour inside their mighty walls.

nobody, absolutely nobody, who can beat Pakhtoon hospitality. A roast chicken is an introduction to breakfast; for lunch, there are several of them, other fowl, and a goat or sheep or two that has been slaughtered in your honour. Half the roasted animal — minus the legs — stands upright on a platter. The meat of other parts is cooked in at least 6 different ways, and appetizingly served. With it goes their wholesome bread in form of huge, flat cakes, and a bit of salad; a vegetable is an insult to a Pathan.

Don't think for a moment that the Pathans must be suffering from high blood pressure or indigestion or the like. The life of the tribal Pathan is so tough that he needs and digests every morsel of it. And they are well built and slim. And you must really eat or your hosts feel offended. They are fast eaters, so try to keep pace. A sweet dish, plenty of fruit and green tea complete the meal.

The Hujra

After the meal you may be shown the mosque at the one side of the courtyard and, as a special honour, the *hujra*, the meeting place or parliament building of the tribal elders. It is dark in there. The fireplace is situated in the middle of the room and the ceiling is black. The room smells of cold ashes. There are mats and cushions on the floor and, of course, the hookahs.

The walls are mostly decorated with the objects of pride and prestige of a Pathan: daggers, knives, rifles, pistols, swords, battle axes... some very old, very famous, very precious, silver hewn, ivory inlaid and worthy of the most prestigious museums — yet functional.

The Khattak Dance

If you have come in a large group, you will now be entertained to Pathan dances, generally called after the most popular one, the Khattak dance. Only the men dance. They dance as groups in circles to the beat of drums. All dances are war-dances, powerful, assertive, arrogant, jubilant, with a rhythm that seems to take root inside you. Their wide, short dance skirts over the billowing shalwars topped by braided, smart waist coats are reminiscent of the Greek costume at the time of the Greek invasion under Alexander the Great, some 2300 years ago.

Behind the Inner Wall

If there is a woman among the visitors she will now be taken to the family section of the killa to greet the women of the clan. The entrance is through a small door in one side of the courtyard.

The male Pathan is one of the most handsome men that walk this earth: tall, well built, masculine and fair, often with blue eyes. While many have the high nose ridge of the classical Greeks, others show the narrow-set eyes and smaller Mongolian features: both are traits of invading forebears.

The Khattak Dance.

With this image of Apollo fresh on your mind you find yourself received by hundreds of women and children, all prepared to meet you. And you find it difficult to believe these are the mothers, sisters and daughters of the Pathan men that you just left at the other side of the wall. The young ones are no doubt pretty, showing the same racial traits. But women look worn and prematurely aged. You must remember that they do all the work: carry large pitchers of water often over long distances, plough the rocky fields and harvest the meagre crop, while their men, rifles in hand, sit at the edge of the field to see that no chance passerby may look in the direction of the working women — else, up comes the rifle! Their birthrate is rising, while healthcare and hygiene remain almost non existent. They dress in long, very wide black cotton dresses over wide shalwars — in the 'good old days' the shalwar was made of 40 metres of cloth! The skin is rough from the smoke of wooden fires and scorching sun, the hands calloused and bony. The normal glance of the black eyes is dulled by a life spent within the high walls or in the toil of the field.

You can see the beauty of Pathan women in the settled areas where women lead a much easier life; the womenfolk of the landlords know how to look after themselves. The result is invariably a picture of classical proportion, grace and highminded features. At their best, the Pathans are next to none in appearance.

In an ocean of little girls and grown women you squeeze through the endless narrow corridors, and left and right and everywhere there are the high mudwalls, with small openings in between. Behind, you see a small courtyard with one or two rooms at the back: the living quarters of the smallest group, a couple with their children, parents, sisters and brothers. Apart from bedsteads, mats, boxes, cooking utensils and transistor radios there is no other furniture.

Tribal Philosophy

The Pathan tribes are often not so poor — indeed, some have recently become very rich as this area grows most of the opium poppies, all hidden behind the walls. They trade in all modern gadgets that they smuggle openly into the country, as well as chocolates, fine soaps and toiletries. All these items are used by the Pathans in the settled areas in the plains. That is why they are looked down upon by the tribal Pathans of the mountains. It is this life of austerity, hardship and frugality, and rejection of all softening luxuries that has given the Pathan the identity that he is proud of.

A GIFT TO TAKE AS A GUEST

Generally a cherished guest will be given a guest-present. It would be appropriate to take a gift along to present on arrival. Considering the Pathan's frugal lifestyle it is often difficult to know what to take. A suitable gift may be a quality picture book of your homeland or anything by way of cloth from there. A Swiss pocket knife is always greatly admired. A lady guest might purchase a good, embroidered shawl for the host's wife. Everybody will appreciate copies of photos that you take there, so ask for the correct address. Leave your camera behind before you enter the women's section of the killa, as women should not be photographed.

— Chapter Six —

THE STREET SCENE

The bazaar is the Pakistani's cultural, social and trading centre in one. His life, his free time is spent there; though nowadays, perhaps a little less in sophisticated urban areas as educated husbands do spend time with their families.

In the bazaar, each man is a spectator and actor at the same time. The tea-stalls, the shop fronts, the street curbs are laden with squatting men in turbans and caps, with beards and weapons, simply dressed or poor, but equally relaxed. They smoke the hookah or plenty of cigarettes, sip green tea, spit, chew betel nut, talk politics and business — and watch. And indeed, the oriental bazaar is so full of

The Friday bazaar reveals the country's unimaginable riches of fruit and vegetables.

human happenings, engaging quarrels, bargaining, win-or-lose situations and of people of all trades and shades that it is a never ending entertainment and fascinating stage-scene.

Shopowners with shawls slung over their shoulders watch over sales boys with an air of fat authority; poor, self-made traders offer knives or plastic toys on a sheet on the pavement to children in torn clothes and with unkempt hair marvelling at the displays; the cart-dealers with fruits or vegetables disappear when the police appear as they have no licence. Blaring loudspeakers attract youths in jeans and leather jackets to the shops and stalls of film-music and cassettes. A sahib, a gentleman, stops at the squatting keymaker's under an umbrella to have a spare key made. Huge legs of beef hang outside butcher's shops in side streets.

The shops in these bazaars are on average the size of a decent wardrobe, each packed to capacity. When the salesman wants to 'enter', he pulls up the shutters, draws out a small table laden with goods, takes his seat on a small stool and then pulls the table back to him. He has everything within easy reach; whatever is piled too high, he will balance within reach with the help of a rod. You can never stand 'in' these shops, only outside them on the pavement. If the shopkeeper does not have what you want, he will yell across the lane to one of his colleagues, or rivals, and have it brought to you from there.

The person who rushes through the bazaar is a loser. He will be served slowly, almost discourteously, and later than others, and may even be offered inferior quality. Authority lies in dignified, slow movement and speech, in taking your time. And it's the air of authority that is respected and served first. The bazaars are often claustrophobic; if you cannot stand crowds or the suffocating heat in them in summer you had better stay away.

Women in Public Life

The street scene has frightened many foreign women — and disappointed foreign men. Used to the anonymity of western street life in which she can relax, the foreign woman finds herself stared at in no uncertain terms. She is helpless there. Staring back or making a scene has the effect of creating more attention and nothing else.

The foreign woman makes an impact in the bazaar by her determined and demanding speech and the money she can afford to spend; but it does not always leave a good impression. By and large, you are quite safe in the bazaar. But if you want to relax, take your servant with you on your shopping spree. It will help in many ways. He can even bargain for you.

THE ORGANISATION OF THE BAZAAR

The bazaar is the oriental shopping system which goes back to antique times. Nowadays, even a small accumulation of shops of different kinds such as a pharmacy, a butcher, and a bakery together is called a bazaar. But the old system was different and is still very much in existence. Many traders selling the same wares set up shops side by side forming a mostly long row, often with sidestreets included. In this way they act like a trade union, they watch each other, and ensure that nobody sells anything at a lower or higher price than the other. Unwritten ethics allow the next shopkeeper to call out to the shopper only when the prospective customer has left the premises of another shop.

Thus, you have cloth bazaars. Some in Lahore and Karachi consist of hundreds of stalls side by side forming narrow lanes under a roof in an area the size of half a football pitch. The variety of cloth, the colours, prints, shades and designs are unbelievable. Both the cloth bazaar and the goldsmith bazaar are the unconquerable reserves of women. Every month, except Muharram and Ramadan, is marriage season and gold-sets worth hundreds of thousands of rupees have to be purchased. The glitter of gold, the sparkle of diamonds and fire of rubies set in traditional oriental designs is something even a very sober, western woman finds hard to resist.

In this way, you have shoe bazaars with modern style shoes alongside displays of gold and silver slippers and sandals, typical Sindhi slippers narrow like a shoe-tree, or men's wedding slippers studded with beads. Then the crockery bazaar, the brass bazaar, the hardware bazaar, the meat and vegetable bazaars, and crowning it all, the carpet bazaar.

There are several old and famous bazaars throughout the country. The Kissakhani Bazaar is famous for its story-telling Pathans; the Dara Bazaar outside Peshawar is a rifle bazaar; and the Bara Bazaar towards the Khyber Pass is a renowned smuggling bazaar.

A typical fish shop.

Other famous bazaars are the bustling, traditional Anarkali Bazaar in Lahore and the Empress Market in Karachi.

Food Stalls

When you enter a meat or fish shop in Pakistan for the first time, you will notice that fish is cut with the foot. The method is neat. There is no science or art in cutting meat, or understanding of the special pieces from various parts of the animal's body; all that is required is to have small pieces for the curry.

The vendor sits on a high platform. After weighing the meat he holds it in both hands before the blade of his knife which he holds between the first and second toe of one foot. The knife remains still, he only moves the meat up and down against the pressure of the

95

knife. The accuracy of the meat-cleaning and cutting proves the expertise. Modern meat- and fish shops have a huge, sabre-like knife fixed on the platform in front of the cutter.

Roti, bread of all kinds, is delicious and it is interesting to watch it being made. It is made of unleavened wheat and the dough is the normal bread dough. Your servant at home will cook the paper-thin *chapatti* on a rimless iron pan. He portions off a bit of dough the size of a peach and beats it between his hands into a thin, flat disc which he then puts on the dry, hot iron pan and bakes it from both sides. The same, but a bit thicker and done in cooking oil is called *parata*. You may also spread mince between two chapatti discs and then fry it in cooking oil.

In the bazaar the professional roti-baker, the *tandoori*, sits on a platform which has a hole in the middle. The hole contains a clay vessel, the *tandoor*, which is about 120 centimetres deep and 1 metre wide under which a coal fire or, in cities, a gas fire is burning. The tandoori makes his cake about 1 centimetre thick, places it on a thickly padded, round hand-pan and hits it on to the hot inner side of the vessel. By the time the walls of the vessel are filled with these *nans*, the first ones are done — they nearly fall off the walls and the tandoori picks them out with a long iron rod with a kind of fishing hook at the end. If you wish, he applies cooking oil on the hot nan. This is then called *roghni roti*; it lasts for many days and is therefore taken on long journeys.

On the weekly holiday people like to sleep late and settle for a brunch. You see small queues outside stalls from which come loud, slapping sounds. Here, the professional *halwa-puriwala* is at work. He has a small ball of wheat-dough in his hands and with these loud, smacking sounds he achieves a paper-thin disc between his hands. With a twist and a whirl he sends the *puri* like a frisby flying into a wide iron pan with boiling oil in it. The discs blow up like hollow balls and hungry families take them home by the dozen along with a bit of the hot spicy lentil or bean dip and some sweet semolina *halwa*. The puriwalas in old city parts vie with each other for the loudest smacks by which their expertise is judged.

Western style bread, almost always white bread for toasting, is called 'double roti'. It is available everywhere.

For those who prefer western food, the country has a wide range of attractive food. There are, to start with, all kinds of packed biscuits. They are excellent. Bakeries, too, offer very good biscuits and all kinds of fine pastry and cakes. Make sure you go to an established bakery. In low income areas the confectionery is cheaper but has more red and green colouring than eggs and butter in it.

The traditional local sweetmeats are called *mit'hia'i*, which many foreigners find too sweet. They are cubes or balls of various colours made of lentil-flour cooked in syrup. *Barfi* is made of thickened milk and when fresh, is very delicious. Also, in the bazaars, you can watch a man holding a small funnel or bag with a hole in the middle over a huge, wide iron pan with a rim. From the hole, he squeezes a pink sugar mix into the hot oil in his pan. He forms bizarre shapes which immediately swell and harden. This *jalebi*, when still warm, is delicious while driving back home but it is not recommended for weight watchers.

These sweets are always distributed on Eids, when a son is born, at birthdays and on every congratulatory or take-along mission. A fine Muslim tradition is that when you have passed an examination, got a job or promotion, had a baby boy or on any other happy occasion, it is you who distribute these sweets as an offering. It is like saying: Please share my joy through these sweets. It is also a kind of thanksgiving. The chocolate industry is still in its initial stages and its products do not yet compare well with others. Toffees and sweets are very good.

The Pan-Wala

Everywhere you will see people with ochre lips and gums or even teeth that seem to have a blackish-red lining. These are the habitual betel nut eaters; actually, the betel leaf is eaten, with a bit of ground nut wrapped in it. The country spends huge amounts of foreign exchange on importing this national delicacy.

The *panwala* squats on a platform surrounded with a variety of small bottles with colourful contents. If you ask him for a 'meet'ha pan', a sweet *pan*, he will take a pre-cut portion of the large leaf and first apply a white paste on it. This is lime. Then follows a red-brown paste. Then the contents of various bottles of red, silver and multicoloured beads, crushed betel nut, tobacco, sugared aniseed, followed by several other ingredients. You may name your choices. The variety and richness of the spreads account for the panwala's fame. The heap is then topped with some liquid syrups and, with a practised twist of his wrist, the panwala manages to fold this small, laden leaf and wrap it in a tight little package. People deposit it deep inside one cheek. It takes quite some time to finish. Slowly the flavours and juices begin to exercise their effect on the tongue.

Foreigners and other beginners often feel uncomfortable with their first pan. It has a strongly astringent effect which makes you feel that the little package is swelling and swelling in your mouth. Yet, it is fun to give it a try. It is said to be good for digestion and is eaten after a meal.

When ladies meet for a ladies' session there will always be some pan 'addicts' among them. You can see it from the boxes they carry with them wherever they go; these are the *pandan*, the pan-boxes. They are of brass or bronze or silver. When you open the lid you find a tray with several small pots in it for the different ingredients while the leaf rests moist in a tissue under the tray. The pandans are beautiful and are often purchased as antiques from the copper bazaars.

Bargaining

Not everybody is a born bargainer. You need a special temperament for it: do not be excitable, or taken in by the vendor's proclamations about his great losses or poverty, do not be affected by the old clothes he wears, and you should be convinced that the article you want to buy is actually cheaper and that the vendor will suffer no loss on your account. Bargaining is a tradition of the east and is vigorously practised in Pakistan. Everyone is trying to make a bargain. It is a game. If you leave a shop with the feeling that they are trying to cheat you by quoting you such high rates you are the loser on all counts: you could have got the articles more cheaply if you had tried; and you leave a bad impression for not being cultured enough to follow the rules and play the game.

Generally, when you protest about the quoted rate some salesmen will ask you to speak up and make your offer so that the game may start. When it comes to big items such as carpets, the game may last for days, like cricket. You sit pensively for hours nodding your head discussing this or that and, at the appropriate moment, coming back to the price issue. You begin to know each other's families and problems. Some spoken Urdu will be of great help. Except for groceries and foodstuffs, things here are not sold at fixed prices. A sale without bargain is a transaction devoid of feeling. People are very emotional and, in trading, emotions run high. Words would be loud when you feel you are near the goal, tempers hot till the moment of agreement, of disengagement with the feeling of victory on both sides.

Even the boy at the road-crossing who sells three dusters for five rupees expects you to examine his wares, criticise the quality, go through his bundle for better specimen or ask for a different colour before you purchase any. Their expertise is such that the trading lasts exactly as long as the red light on the traffic light. In this sense, people have a perfect sense of time. And it is the norm, not the exception, to have a conversation during a deal.

You need to learn at what price you should begin to make your offers. There is only one general rule: the bigger, and the more expensive the item, the lower you may start your quoting. Some people when buying carpets start from 50 per cent lower than the price quoted by the trader. They tell me they get it for that, but I doubt it. 20-30 per cent is a good deal for you. Of course you may start at 50 per cent lower and see where the game takes you. Always remember, it's a game.

The Smells

The bazaar announces itself from a distance by the smell of dust and smoke mingled with sweat. When you enter a shop where meat, fish and live poultry are sold your first reaction might be to flee. Spice shops are enjoyable to see. Traditional shops have no closed fronts so you can reach for the goods to examine them. But when it comes to spice shops you had better keep your distance. The spices are beautifully piled up into pyramids in wide baskets, red, yellow, grey and many more shades, and there are more mysterious powders and crooked sticks in tins and drawers. They are a world by themselves: from highly fragrant herbs to intoxications to giddying pungencies. And if you are tempted to examine the beautiful red powder pile, you will be rewarded with a prolonged sneezing fit: it is chilli powder, although not pure, as everything is adulterated, but nevertheless beautiful.

All old bazaars have open drains, an amazing and very pungent mini-world of their own.

Your Daily Shopping

Every locality has its own small bazaar or markets for your daily needs. It will take some days and efforts till your grocer or baker is convinced you are not the type trying to boss and play superior. You prove it to him by trying your Urdu on him, by asking him the Urdu word for this or that and let yourself be corrected by him. But don't ignore checking the bill, that's when the air of authority is required. After a few days you will feel that he is beginning to trust you. He will then not overcharge and give you good and fresh food items.

Every city has deep freeze shops where foreigners prefer to buy choice meat which is cut to suit western cooking. Normally you do not get a bill. You may ask for one if you need one — it's not a problem. Do not ask for pork, ham or bacon as you cannot get it anywhere. All meat that is sold is halal, slaughtered in the way prescribed by the Koran. Dry cleaners are quite inexpensive and good. They normally also wash clothes in normal washing machines. All ironing is excellent. Medicine shops are easily found and well stocked with foreign medicines.

When you go to a shop or office where other people are waiting you will be surprised that you are asked immediately about your wishes. Don't imagine for a minute that you are given preferential treatment. It seems to be quite a system that the one who enters last gets the attention and service first; so much so that some expatriates who were in the middle of their business with an official left the room when others entered and interfered, only to re-enter immediately and be the last — and be served first once more! It is said to have taught a lesson here and there. In shops, it is common for someone to enter briskly, and loudly demand this or that. The salesman will leave you alone, particularly if you have a longer shopping list and attend to the newcomer.

It is then useful to voice your demands energetically or leave the shop in protest. But, since in the next-door shop you will run into the same situation it may be better just to pretend to be leaving or your shopping won't get done that morning.

In contrast to the game of the bargaining procedure in the bazaar, many salesmen are by and large unfriendly; they never smile, they display their wares unwillingly, talk to others in between and seem to be making an effort to be rude. This behaviour appears to be deliberate and probably finds its explanation in the fact that in the social structure of the Sub-continent, the merchant is of a lower class. In his way, the salesman feels he is the boss.

In trading places which can be called establishments you find the same commercial smiles as everywhere in the world.

Places to Eat

Food is something all Pakistanis love. Again, there are stark contrasts in food intake: you may find a labourer having just an onion with a nan, and then see three or six dishes served at a small dinner party. There are wasteful cooking and eating practices. Cooking is such that most vitamins and minerals are destroyed. Also, Pakistani food is very greasy as too much oil is used for cooking. The base of a curry consists of onions and tomatoes cooked with meat and spices in oil. Sometimes at wedding feasts, a poorer host may put an extra can of oil in the cooking pot to serve as a deterrent from over eating.

Hawkers sell a delicious variety of quick snacks or cheap meals from their wheel carts. In winter in any bazaar, you can see a hawker selling chicken soup from a huge pot on his cart over which is suspended a solitary skinned chicken. I have watched such chickens and come to the conclusion that they last throughout the winter in this upside down position and never get any closer to the brew in the pot! Maybe the steam that touches them brings the flavour to the soup. Next are the *chats*. These are either a mixture of fruit or of gram flour prepared in different ways and served with a spicy gravy and yoghurt. There is at least one hawker outside every school at the end of the day. Another popular food is the *bun kebab*, the local version of a hamburger. The meat patty is prepared in an egg mix and fried and served between the cut bun. Then, we come to the *chola*. These are grams that have been boiled with chillies and salt and are served with a tamarind based gravy. These are some of the favourite quick foods sold by roadside hawkers.

Also, for about six months in a year the *sita-wala* is a target of all passers-by and schoolchildren. *Sita* are whole maize-cobs that are either boiled and rubbed with lemon and sprinkled with chilli powder and salt or roasted in hot ashes. They are wholesome and loved by young and old.

MEALS

Nihari derives its name from the Urdu word *nihar,* which means morning. After one nihari breakfast you certainly do not need any other food for the rest of the day and, after reading its description you might prefer to stick to your cornflakes and toast.

Chunks of fatty beef each weighing about 100g are cooked overnight in a huge metal pot in cooking oil, chillies and a variety of other spices. After waking up, you eat it with nan. For a little extra money you can get portions of bone marrow, brain, kidney or liver added to it. It is a sure cure for heavy eyes and sultry stomachs, as after having a plate of it you are wide awake and your stomach is on overtime.

Halwa-Puri is a slightly lighter breakfast favourite and has already been described. An average Punjabi can polish off six of these oil dripping puris and, if he is really hungry, he consumes up to fifteen of these.

Parata is a more common food for breakfast which can also be made at home. It is a flat cake fried in oil. It is eaten with omelette or fried egg.

With these staple foods there is a choice of drinks of which tea is the most common, a kind of national drink. Rural people often drink a glass of milk if they can afford, or *lassi.* This is yoghurt mixed with water and ice crumbs flavoured with sugar for breakfast and mostly with salt for lunch. It is an ideal drink in summer as it has a cooling effect. In summer you find it being prepared at every corner of a bazaar. In Lahore, it is served in litre glasses and a piece of thickened sweet cream is added to give it body.

After a hearty breakfast we turn our attention of course to lunch. Here, the variety is unlimited. Here are a few of the most common dishes.

In Karachi, *korma* is a favourite dish. This is a thick gravy of meat or chicken. *Behari kebab* is mince tied to a skewer and grilled over charcoal. When it is served, you spend the better part of the

103

meal trying to untangle the thread around the meat and might end up getting entangled yourself. Another variety of kebab is called *gola kebab*. It resembles the behari kebab only it lacks the thread. Then, there is a large variety of south Indian foods like sour brinjals. And if you still have not had your fill of chillies you can find a dish of chilli-curry anywhere.

Three famous dishes are found in Quetta. Because of the desolate and barren countryside the main foods are all meat based. *Sajji* is a whole lamb that has been skinned and salted, then put in an oven to bake. The meat is ready after about eight hours, tender and extremely delicious. *Tikkas* are pieces of mutton that are put on a skewer and roasted over a charcoal grill. 'Joints' are thick chunks of mutton cooked with only salt and pepper. All these dishes are served with piping hot nans. With most meals goes a dish of yoghurt that dilutes the effect of grease and chillies. Fresh mixed salad comes with every meat dish.

In Lahore, try *Paya*, either goat or cow trotters that are cooked in a thick gravy and served with nan. The gelatine is so thick in it that after eating about two goat trotters, your fingers get glued together. *Murgh Chola* is chicken cooked with grams. It is again a very delicious dish with plenty of spices in it. Here however I must mention that the spices are not added with the same vigour as they are in Karachi, so you may find the food more palatable. *Gajar ka halwa* is a sweet prepared from carrots and sugar with pieces of dried sweetened cream mixed in it. This is a winter sweet as the carrots are in season then. It is served piping hot from a huge iron pan.

Peshawar is known for its *chapli kabab* and *karhai*. In Urdu a chapli means a shoe and a chapli kabab on average is the size of the sole of a shoe. It consists of mince made into a pancake and has salt, chillies, dried pomegranate seeds and an egg added to it. It is fried in an open flat frying pan in sheep's fat. *Karhai* are pieces of meat that are cooked with salt and tomatoes in a deep frying pot with very little oil.

People take care to wash their hands before and after a meal. This may also include a noisy cleaning of the mouth and throat.

There will be many other dishes for you to taste and be surprised about. Pakistani cooking is a great art, though slightly mystifying for the understanding of a foreigner as it takes many hours to cook one curry.

Chapter Seven

THE LIFE CYCLE

In any society the birth, marriage and death of a human being have an impact, and it is the same in Pakistan. What will surprise you most about the ceremonies that are conducted on these occasions is the lavish arrangements that are made. The religious injunction for simplicity is nowhere to be found, a false status is maintained.

THE CHILD IS BORN

The birth of a male heir is heralded with pride and often rifle shots, which at times may stretch beyond the means of the poor parents. But the parents feel that the heir will look after his parents in their old age and so from the day he is born, he is pampered and spoiled. A daughter is a burden and the parents take her as a responsibility that they have to live with. This archaic thinking has hardly changed among the poor people of this country and even the educated are not free of it. You will generally hear from parents how desperately they are looking for a suitable match, to marry off their daughter. The responsibility for a daughter ends with her wedding.

When a son is born in a family, the father will rush off to a sweetmeat shop and buy *luddus*, a sweet that is distributed at the birth of the child. These sweets are packed into little colourful boxes, and the father will go to the homes of all his relatives and friends and distribute the sweets personally and announce the arrival of his heir. The friends and relatives respond by visiting the proud parents, admiring the heir and placing some money in the hands of the child. Happiness must be shared so, if the parents can afford it, they will get some food cooked and distribute it among the poor. If he happens to be the first child in the family, the parents will do all they can to guard him against all illnesses. If the mother is a religious person and has been praying for the birth of a son at the shrine of a saint, she will rush off there as soon as she is able to and thank the saint for her good fortune, and will take a gift of sweets or a set of clothes to give to the keeper of the shrine. She will also get a *ta'weez* (a sacred charm to protect the child against all evil) from a saintly person (you would be surprised at the number of such saintly persons that exist in this country) to tie around the child's arm and neck. Most children wear such charms throughout their lives and strongly believe in their protecting powers.

When the child, be it male or female, is born, the first sound it is supposed to hear is the Muslims' call for prayer (the azan). The honour of reciting this to the child is given to the eldest male member of the family or the *maulvi* who is specially called in for this occasion. The first thing that the child is supposed to taste is honey, mixed with a bit of pure butter fat which is shaped into tiny balls and then put carefully into the new-born child's mouth.

The arrival of a daughter is not heralded with the same signs of happiness as that of a son. In fact the father is apologetic in his announcement. Sweets are distributed but on a limited scale. A daughter is treated as a second class citizen from the day she arrives. She does all the menial work for the family and helps her mother in the household. The parents try to save from their meagre means to get a suitable dowry together to marry the daughter off. Her opinion is never asked. Schooling will only be provided if the parents can afford it. So it is not a happy lot that a daughter finds herself in, in this country. Even the well-to-do think that their ultimate responsibility is finding a suitable match for their daughter. Very few women have been able to break out of these chains and find careers of their choice. Even till this day there are very few women who find employment.

You as a foreigner can give a suitable gift to the new born and congratulate the proud parents.

CIRCUMCISION

This is an important ceremony in the life of a Muslim boy, and is traditionally performed when the child is 2 to 5 years old. Nowadays this task is performed by the doctor on the newborn baby while the mother and child are still in the hospital. But this is only true for the educated class. The illiterate and poorer class still believe in having this ceremony performed when the child is older.

The whole family or village is invited for the ceremony. A huge meal is prepared by the village barber, who is the chef on all occasions and is also responsible for performing the circumcision. Yes, the local barber is a very talented person and does far more than give hair cuts and shaves. The child is dressed in his best clothes that may be specially made for the occasion. After all the guests have gathered the child is brought out by the father, and in front of the entire gathering, the barber performs the task. The child is wrapped up and returned to the mother for solace, while the guests are invited to partake in the feast. The guests on departing give some money to the child. In more educated families, the feast is held at any suitable time after the actual circumcision has taken place.

MARRIAGES

Marriage is traditionally less the bonding of two people than the bonding of two families. In some parts of the country a child's bride or groom is chosen even before the child is born. Inter marriages among the family and the community are quite common. That is why engagements may be formalised when they are babies or children without any formal ceremony. But, for those whose fates have not been decided at the time of birth or by the family elders, the village midwife, who is also the village gossip and match-maker, is given the task of finding a suitable match. If there happens to be no midwife in the village the barber takes on this role. All negotiations regarding the dowry are carried out by the go-between. In most cases, the would-be bride and groom are then shown a photo of each other. Until recently and, perhaps even now in remote areas, the couple see each other for the first time during the wedding ceremonies when a mirror is placed between them. This allows the bride to keep her eyes lowered modestly. In cities, often young couples now see each other face to face before they take the vows. In rare cases, they are allowed to go out together; if so then mostly in the company of others.

If a daughter or son disapproves of the choice, the parents will usually give in. Marrying off one's children is a very delicate matter and might leave whole families embarrassed or insulted if the proposed match does not work out.

When a girl reaches the age of 18 in the countryside and 24 in cities, it is almost too late for marriage. This makes some parents lose their sleep and health. Marriages are often arranged, and neither the boy nor the girl has much say in the choice of his or her life partner. In Islam, marriage is a social contract which each partner has to fulfil — on the one side, earning bread, protecting the family and providing for their needs; and on ther other, obedience to male superiority, providing sexual satisfaction, rearing children, keeping a home and looking after the husband's property. Love is not an issue, and it may or may not arise during marriage. It often does. But since it is a very personal and intimate thing, it is not exposed to the public eye or talked about.

The Dowry

The overwhelming problem for parents in the lowlands of Pakistan is the dowry. This is generally up to the bride's parents, though in the western parts and among some tribes, they follow the Persian system where the boy has to give the bride money. This is another example of the earlier Hindu influence. Traditionally, 99 sets of clothes and several sets of jewellery (heavy long necklaces, rings, earrings and bracelets of pure gold) were the standard demand. Now, the list is extended by a fridge, a TV, an air-conditioner, a car, house, lands... The marriage ceremonies last for three days on average and for these days the bride's father has to feed hundreds of guests and accommodate all those who come from far away. In addition, all senior in-laws expect him to give them expensive gifts of suiting and jewellery.

The show is condemned by everybody as it ignores the Islamic tenets. But everyone tries to produce an even bigger show. The poor take loans to get their daughters married, which they cannot pay back in a lifetime and which has often resulted in bonded labour.

Women's social aid groups stitch, embroider and collect to make trousseaus ready for orphan girls in orphanages so that they may be able to marry. When a daughter is born, wise mothers secretly begin to put aside a rupee a day in order to survive the wedding D-day.

Wedding Preparations

Once a suitable match has been found, the wedding preparations start. The most auspicious date for the wedding is chosen, often in consultation with a religious person. It is debated whether the ceremonies should be held at home — inclusive of the neighbours' gardens and the stretch of road in front of the house — or in a wedding hall. It is the girl's parents who have to carry the biggest burden during the marriage. Most of the ceremonies associated with a marriage are not Muslim, but traditional to the Sub-continent. It is only the *nikka,* the legalising of the marriage, that is Muslim.

The girl's mother starts by buying and preparing the wedding dress for the bride to wear on the Walima (see page 118), as well as ordering clothes for the bridegroom, and at times for his parents and brothers and sisters as well. She also puts the dowry in order: boxes full of dresses and unstitched clothes, several sets of jewellery, and household items are the minimum. The girl's friends meet many days before the wedding, and every evening at the girl's house and sing wedding songs accompanied by the beat of a drum. The house wears a festive look. If the family can afford it, hundreds of coloured bulbs illuminate the house and remain on during the entire period of the wedding.

The boy's family also start their preparations. The bridal dress and jewellery, which the bride wears on the actual wedding day, are ordered. Usually the family's jewels are taken out and polished, and are passed on to the bride of the heir. The bridegroom is not allowed to visit or to see his bride till they are wed. It is not uncommon to find that the bride and groom have never met each other till their wedding.

The Mehndi Ceremony

A day before the actual wedding, the *mehndi* ceremony is performed. A week before this ceremony is to take place the bride is rubbed with oil, and she may not bathe till just before the mehndi

The henna is applied to the bride's hands while she sits through the ceremony in veiled modesty.

ceremony takes place. The drums now do not cease beating. The marriage festival starts with this ceremony. The bride is dressed in a beautiful dress, which is simple, and made to sit on a little stool surrounded by her friends and relatives. She has to sit with her head bowed down, and cannot look directly at anyone. The friends sing wedding songs.

And then the bridegroom is brought in by his family and friends. It is the peak moment of this joyous and exciting celebration. Everyone in the bride's party starts whispering such comments as 'Oh he is handsome! His nose is too long! He should be thinner! Oh, and so tall!' His sisters and other female relatives bring in the henna that is to be applied to the bride's hands. The henna comes in the form of a paste on a round tray, decorated with tinsel.

'Mehndi' is the Urdu word for the Arabic 'henna'. The colouring of hands and feet expresses joy. The girl who carries it starts gyrating till all the groom's female party dances before the bride, singing and swinging the henna tray on which a circle of candles is burning. It is accompanied by baskets full of sweetmeats for the bride's family, who respond by beckoning the guests to a lavish feast spread on long rows of tables. The bridegroom's sisters sing their songs and the bride's sisters and friends respond with theirs.

There is usually a lot of bantering that goes on between the two parties, as they ridicule each other. The girls then get together and start dancing traditional group dances and the other family members and friends are also pulled into the dancing that goes on till the early hours of the morning. The henna is applied to the bride's hands by the groom's sisters and mother, though not usually directly on the hands but on a leaf that covers the palms. As soon as the ceremony is over the bride removes the henna from her hands as later, one of her friends or a professional will apply the henna in delicate floral designs on her hands and feet.

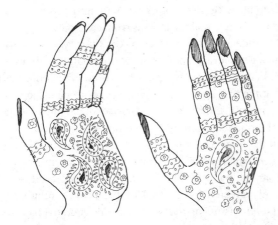

The Wedding

On the following day, the wedding itself is more a formal, but lavish feast. Many hotels cater for them. Parks, playgrounds, wedding halls or hotels are the venue; in villages the village square, streets and courtyards of neighbours. There the barber steps in again as the cook for the wedding. In Karachi you will find streets full of marriage halls.

All marriages are sumptuous affairs that usually leave the bride's parents in debt. The foreigner is struck by the extravagance of the meals and the amount of dowry that is given. Rather than just starting the newly weds on the road of a married life, they are given all the amenities that they might need: a house, TV, refrigerator, furniture, cooking utensils, clothes, money, car. The list can be endless.

Remember no wedding starts on time, therefore you can afford to be late. 9.30 p.m. is a safe time to get to a wedding even if the card says 8.00 p.m. sharp. Men, women and children are all invited. The actual solemnising of the wedding, the religious ceremony, may take place before the reception. This depends on what has been agreed upon by the two families. A maulvi provides the religious sanction while two male witnesses from each party sign the document after the bride and groom have spoken their 'yes'. The *nikka-nama*, the marriage contract, spells out the contract, the divorce rights and financial commitments in case of divorce. This contract is usually signed at the bride's home or in a side room near the wedding hall.

The bride's family are the first to reach the marriage venue, where the bride is taken to a side room where she is made to sit and wait till the marriage papers are prepared. The bridegroom's party, the *barat*, which often runs into hundreds of guests and may be accompanied by a band playing traditional wedding songs, is elaborately greeted by a panel of the bride's relatives. After the nikka (solemnising of the wedding) has taken place the bride is brought in to the reception hall by her sisters and friends. Modesty

The bridegroom signs the nikka-nama, the marriage contract, in the presence of the mullah, the male witnesses and friends. The bride signs the document in another room.

prescribes that her head be bent and a heavy brocade sheet just leaves her eyes uncovered.

She is led slowly towards the stage where her husband is sitting waiting for her. It may be the heavy clothes and jewellery that she is wearing on this special day, or the fears of what lies ahead of her in married life that hamper her progress towards the man she has just married.

The groom, dressed up in his own wedding dress, which is

115

The newly-weds sit together on the stage and face their guests.

usually a traditional silk long coat or a western suit, sits on the sofa on the stage and gets up to greet his bride. He may wear the *sahra* over his face. This is a flower or tinsel curtain that is tied on the groom's head and covers his eyes and face, but this custom has now mostly receded to village environments.

As soon as the bride sits on the stage next to the bridegroom, the families surround her, the photographers move in and start clicking away. With the invention of the video camera, this menace has taken over the still-camera's job. The spool runs from the very beginning and keeps the couple in focus with the bright lights and silent movie, right through the whole ceremony. After the family photographs have been taken, people start going up to congratulate and bless the newly-weds. The friends of the bride meanwhile try hard to deprive the groom of one shoe; he has to pay heavily, often hundreds of rupees, to get it back. Some time during these proceedings dinner will be announced. The news spreads like wild fire and everyone abandons the bridal couple and moves towards the food. Don't be shocked at the jostling, shoving and pushing that you will experience at the dinner table, which is usually a buffet. Everyone attacks the food table as if it is the last meal he is going to get and in a matter of minutes the food has disappeared from the table. A team of harangued waiters clears up the mess. The bridal couple gets a dinner table set up before them on the stage.

After the dinner people start departing, leaving the family to carry on. The newly-weds sit through it all, and don't mix with the guests. Finally it is time for the bride to leave with her husband. It is a tearful and solemn moment for the bride when, under a copy of the Holy Koran held over her head, she leaves behind all that she has known and loved and steps into the shiny, tinsel bedecked car to be driven to an uncertain future.

In the village, the bride sits in a *doli* (palanquin) and is carried on a horse or camel to the groom's house. In cities, the cultural rift is such that the traditional doli may be standing ready next to the black Mercedes, both richly decorated. Horse and doli are then mostly ignored in favour of the limousine.

If you happen to attend a village marriage, don't admire the vegetables that may be growing in the fields next to the marriage venue. Someone did that once, and the lunch was delayed as the cook (village barber) was asked to cook the vegetables. It is a matter of honour for the bride's family to provide for any request that may be made by the groom's guests.

The Walima

A day or two after the wedding the bridegroom's parents host a reception: the *walima*. This is to honour the consummating of the marriage. This is again a lavish spread, and will of course not start at the time mentioned on the invitation. In fact, if one were to get there on time, even the hosts would not be there. All the guests assemble and the bride and groom again sit on a stage in their fineries with the cameraman throwing the spotlight on them and filming away. They again don't mix with the guests and it is again the guests who go up and congratulate them. This is of course until dinner is announced, at which everyone abandons them and goes off to eat. The walima is usually a shorter and much more sober reception. Modern urban couples follow the western custom of honeymooning. There is no word for it in Urdu, as the framework of the agricultural background of the country work and duty continues the day after the walima.

Gifts

Bridal gifts are basically the same the world over. For household or personal use, everything is welcome. From a foreigner, items that come from abroad are most highly appreciated. If you are close to the bridegroom's family, a household item may be useful. You get good thermos flasks, beautiful cushions, table linen or decorative pieces in the country, or a tie or shirt. If you are a friend of the bride's party, also cosmetics, perfumes or a length (5 metres or so) of silk cloth are customary gifts. Flowers are not regarded as gifts. You must attach a greeting card with your name to your gift as you have to hand it over to an appointed female relative of the bride and boxes will be opened several days later. Often lists are made with the names of the donors and the items for a proper 'thank-you' card or adequate reciprocation at any later occasion.

OTHER FESTIVE OCCASIONS

Other commemorative days like the birthday of adults or wedding anniversaries are not observed. However urban folks who want to be 'modern' often celebrate these occasions, and in no small way.

MARRIED LIFE

Almost every girl is brought up with the aim of marriage as the ultimate destiny of her life. The age-old prerequisites for finding and keeping a husband are instilled into her from early childhood: modesty; not answering back; rearing his children; sacrificing for the family; accepting him as he is, even if he brings other women into the house; and most importantly, to obey the future mother-in-law. It is this last point which causes untold misery to young wives, sometimes even resulting in their deaths. But when they, in turn, attain the position of a mother-in-law, they often play the same role; it is the only time that they find themselves in the position of command.

The Pakistani male is, by western standards, totally spoilt. Where in the West he washes dishes, takes over household chores and caters to babies' and children's needs, the Pakistani husband will do no such things. If one in a thousand should be emancipated enough to do such tasks they will be done unseen or he will be laughed at by his friends and colleagues. Even if the wife is working, she is expected to take full charge of the household. In the upper middle class, household servants are then a great relief.

On top of it the husband needs to be personally attended to. The wife has to pour him the tea and serve it to him, she will cook his favourite dishes or cook the way he likes things to be cooked and not the way others like it. He will help himself first at the table. He expects to find his shoes polished and in the right place, the hot water ready and the clothes laid out. In short, a good wife pampers her husband, is patient, does not press a point and does not answer back; she treats him like her lord and master.

In most cases, the husband spends much of his free time outside the home in the company of his friends. Sitting with his wife the whole day would be a matter of ridicule and non-comprehension to them. But where there is educated partnership between husband and wife, the husband does spend time at home — and nobody will

119

question it. Even the simplest man feels that there is a meaning to it.

Before marriage, the girl is the property of her parents; after marriage she belongs to her husband and her in-laws. The young girl becomes a possession of the family of her husband; he often has less say in matters regarding his wife than his mother, whom he too has to obey. The only way for a young wife to attain recognition is by giving birth to sons since this establishes her virtue. She is blessed by God. The woman, particularly if she already has daughters, goes through untold agony before the birth of the next child, but if that again is a girl, people commiserate with her, and she must be prepared for the worst in case there is no male offspring: divorce. This also happens in case of infertility: it is no one but the woman who is at fault.

Four Wives

A poor woman such as this with no children breathes a sigh of relief if her husband under such circumstances, marries a second, third or even fourth wife without throwing her to the ignominious fate of a divorced woman; in remote areas she, thus dishonoured, will not even be received back by her own parents. She is ill-fated and has brought shame to them.

Islam allows a man to have four wives side by side. Often, when the first wife does not bear him a son, the man marries a second wife; even a third, but that is very rare, and I have hardly ever heard of a fourth wife. That would be too expensive and troublesome a venture for most men!

Sometimes a man falls in love with a woman for the first time in his life after his arranged marriage has gone stale. He then might marry that woman. Or, he may feel that his first wife has become too old for him, as often women age prematurely due to hard labour. In most such situations, the wives live under the same roof, and peacefully side by side. The Koran enjoins upon a man to do equal justice to his wives. When the growing children of the various wives see

their father take his pillow from bedroom to bedroom every other night they know that he is doing just that.

Position of Command

Even if the first wife is no longer considered compatible by her husband, this retired wife is not altogether unhappy about her husband's subsequent marriages (provided she has children): she is the senior wife and enjoys a position of command over the other wives and over all their children. While those children call her *bhi-amma* (also-mother) or *buri-amma* (senior mother), the other wives will do what she orders them to do.

In Pathan tribal society which is egalitarian (for men), women do the job that elsewhere sweepers do. And the retired wife in this society finds comfort in the fact that she now does not have to carry the water from the well or empty the bucket! Generally it's the first wife who controls the household money and it's she who, next to her husband, has the greatest say in any decision regarding any or all

121

of the children. Little wonder that many parents — particularly those in rural areas — are set against obtaining any form of higher education for their daughters.

The Married Daughter

In modern city life, the married daughter relates to her own family in quite a normal manner except that even there, she belongs to the husband's family and has to give them precedence in all matters. It is they who would give the name to a baby; they may insist on certain dress styles and decide whether she should observe purdah. She always has to be submissive. Her own parents are like frequent and much loved guests. She may visit them any time she gets permission to do so. At the time of the birth of a child, the wife will spend four to eight weeks with her own mother.

In conservative Pathan circles however, the wife's parents do not visit the daughter unless they are formally invited there. In the minds of some traditionalists it looks improper for the father to stay overnight with his married daughter if he comes from far away. So far, it is all quite understandable and acceptable but it is a shock for a Westerner to see a Pathan father cover his head in shame on the day of his daughter's wedding.

DEATH

The message of somebody's death is conveyed by a personal messenger, or by telephone. Everyone has to be informed within a few hours by whatever means possible. Everyone who comes to know about it gathers at the house of the deceased. Chairs or a rug are spread outside the house for the guests to sit and wait.

The body is given a bath by a religious person, or anyone who knows the rites. The ankles and toes are tied together, the jaw is tied up. The body is perfumed with rose water and wrapped in the coffin cloth. This is a long white piece of cotton similar to what the hajis wear when they perform haj. Rose petals are spread all over the coffin. The body is then placed on a bed (charpoi) and taken to the women's enclosure. Holy verses are recited. Everyone waits till all the near and dear ones have arrived and had a last look at the deceased.

If there is a fear of the body decomposing before all the relatives have arrived, a family elder takes the decision to have the burial rites performed. Otherwise, in summer, ice blocks and fans may be placed around the body. The Koran is distributed in chapter sections which the religious persons among the mourners read quietly or mumble. Many pray with a rosary or pick beans from a basket which serve as rosaries.

At the time of burial the body on its charpoi is carried on the shoulders of all the males who are present, in turn. The women are not allowed to accompany the body for burial, and stand in the door more disconsolate than consoling each other. In case of the death of a small child the father will carry the body in his arms.

In a mosque or open ground or at the cemetery, the last prayers are offered. The body is placed in front of the congregation and a religious person, generally the priest, will recite the last prayers. This prayer is spoken while standing up at the open grave. Everyone is allowed to have a look at the deceased for the last time. Then the face is covered and the body is lowered into the grave. The relatives throw in hands full of earth till the grave is entirely covered. The grave diggers help by shovelling the earth in. The grave is covered with rose petals and other flowers. It is also sprinkled with rose water, and sweet smelling joss sticks are lit. A last prayer is offered after which everyone leaves the graveyard. The women visit the grave site later.

In the house of the deceased, no food is prepared for three days. Friends and relatives provide all the necessary meals for the bereaved family and guests. On the third day, the family and relatives gather again at the house of the deceased and recite verses from the Holy Koran. Food is served to the guests on this occasion. The close relatives of the family visit the grave and offer prayers there.

The period of mourning is forty days. There is no official dress that is worn during the last rites. It is assumed that everyone came as soon as he received the news and did not get time to change. The traditional mourning colour is white but any simple dress is accepted. The dupatta is a must and women keep their heads covered when they are in the house of the deceased.

Chapter Eight

SETTLING IN: YOUR NEW ENVIRONMENT

HOUSE-HUNTING

For some, house-hunting is a nightmare; for others an excitement.
You can run into both situations here irrespective of your personal
inclinations. There are many pages of estate agents in the *Yellow
Pages* of the telephone directory. Unless some have been recommended to you, try some that are situated within the locality where
you intend to live. They also advertise in the English dailies.

In all cities there are plenty of empty houses. Karachi is the only
city that has good flats as well. Accept right from the start that there

are no small houses — they are all big. Rentals are calculated in terms of the number of bedrooms. If you are lucky you can find a three-bedroom house: one for you, one for guests (everyone has guests here) and one is needed as a store-room or study. If you see a house smaller than that the reason is that the owner did not have the money to build a bigger one; its quality is accordingly lower. Those few, two-bedroom jewels are always occupied by the owners themselves.

Expatriates generally take four- to five- bedroom houses. The rents are high, and overheads tremendous but since house-owners know that expatriates can afford it, the rent in all cities has skyrocketed.

Be Watchful!

There are certain danger areas which you must look out for before you close a deal:

1. Knock at all the woodwork in the house to make sure it is not hollowed out by termites.

2. Open drain lids to see how badly the house is infested by cockroaches.

3. Check the gas and electric meters and note the reading and have it signed by the agent; otherwise you may find the last few thousand rupees that your predecessor has not paid smuggled onto your first bill.

4. Thoroughly check the working and condition of geyser, cooker and heaters.

5. See that the roof has adequate insulation, otherwise you can use the upper storey as an oven in summer.

6. Check that there are a sufficient number of power fuses for your air-conditioners.

7. Clearly establish in the contract the lessor's responsibilities.

8. Do not give any money in advance unless all the repairs, paintwork and so forth agreed upon prior to your moving in are

actually executed. Do not even accept the deal of moving into one room with kitchen because they are ready, or else, the rest will never get done.

SETTING UP HOME

Foreigners who know about the good Pakistani furniture arrive with a small amount of luggage and buy all their furniture here. It is exquisite, and a good buy, provided you understand something about it and can point out bad spots or finishes. Do make sure you order furniture from a company that has a wood drying plant.

Curtain cloth is very beautiful, quite cheap and in plenty. Shops supply tailors who sew and fit the curtains in your home. Do be attentive when it comes to calculating the length of cloth for your given requirements in case the shopkeeper sells you several unnecessary extra metres which then quietly disappear during the stitching. Linen and towels are beautiful and of best quality. As for carpets, you are in paradise here.

What to Bring

Bring air-conditioners, fridge, freezer, voltage stabilizer, all electric kitchen gadgets, washing machine, TV, music systems, computer, crockery and cutlery with you from overseas. You can buy all these items here, but they are much more expensive. Don't forget bicycles (in Islamabad and Lahore, for exercise purposes) and the car.

The Miraculous Telephone

There are no public telephone booths in Pakistan. If you need to call up somebody you may ask at a larger shop that is likely to have a telephone connection, a hotel or office. Normally, you can make a short call from there and pay the amount due; often, this is rejected. At other places, you pay double.

You most certainly want and need a telephone connection at your house. In order to use it you must be prepared to sacrifice

127

several hours of your day, and if you are a nervous person, several years of your life. You must learn to speak in competition with several other voices simultaneously, to hear rudeness and, if you are a woman, obscenities, or get such calls in the middle of the night, be an angel of patience and accept inflated bills. It can take many attempts at dialling to get through and often you will hear other people's conversations too or be cut off during a call.

Hire and Fire

From the day your chosen house shows signs of activity people will come pouring in to offer their services as cooks, bearers, gardeners, guards, washermen, ayahs and sweepers. Many will show you recommendations. Your basic needs are a cook, a sweeper and a gardener cum guard.

A cook who comes to the house of a foreigner will insist that there should also be a bearer. If you have many representational and social duties — for example as a diplomat or frequent business entertaining — well and good. Otherwise you don't need one. The more normal choice is a cook who, apart from cooking, also irons and dusts the house of an average family of four. Sometimes these servants are also prepared to sweep the rooms and clean the bathrooms for foreigners, but this requires extra wages. The advantage is that you have fewer people running around your house. The disadvantage is that when this servant goes on leave you are doubly stuck. On average, a family goes through one to two servants before they find one that suits them.

Servants

Right from the start servants should be shown and explained their areas of duty. Generally, servants are not used to working by a set schedule but by orders shouted now and then. Also, it is often new to them to work for a household instead of serving a person. Unless you are lucky to take over a trained servant from another foreigner, you may find that he is very servile but really cannot see the accumulated dust on the sideboard. The housewife needs to invest several hours a day for a week or two when a new servant enters the home. Directions are to be repeated frequently before they become routine. It is laborious but, in the long run, pays off. Later, you only need to supervise and inspect work for short times and you avoid anger, scolding, firing, heartburn, suspicion, tantrums and many bad days.

Say everything loudly and clearly and with polite authority. Make servants repeat your order to make sure they have understood you. Some very religious servants break their work for prayers at the prescribed times. While it is important for them to fulfil their religious duties, there is no need for them to go to the mosque for praying. Only the Friday midday prayers are traditionally said in congregation in a mosque. A servant normally gets one day's holiday per week (Christians on a Sunday, Muslims on a Friday), and about one month off during a year. There are, however, great variations also in the distribution of these holidays. The leave must be discussed with them at the time of hiring.

An untrained servant may consider half a spoon of red chilli powder in a sauce as unspiced. In order to achieve the taste you require, from the start you should instruct or show your servant what spices you need in your soup and which he may keep for himself.

Tea in Pakistan is not really tea unless it is black: again show your servant on the first day how light you want it. If you ask him to bring oranges after lunch, you might get them cut into four or eight pieces on a plate. This is the traditional way of eating oranges, sucking the juice out of the squares. It's pleasant. What you might not like is that he has probably sprinkled salt over the squares and maybe pepper too. Once you get used to that you will probably refuse to eat oranges without salt ever again as it brings out their real flavour. Peaches and pears are eaten likewise. The additional intake of salt, particularly in summer, is very important, especially if you suffer from low blood pressure. And on fruit, it's one of the most tasty ways to supplement your salt intake. Some people also put salt in their tea.

Do be careful when employing and instructing servants to speak with friendly authority! The more softness you show for tales of woe and headaches or people sick back home, the more trouble there will be for you on future occasions. It is also wise to lock away tempting items such as money or jewellery when your servants are in the house.

When a servant has erred, it is better that the man of the house speaks to him than the lady. That would be difficult for him to accept. One thing is very important: never take any subordinate to task in the presence of others. The loss of face for him is very severe and you may lose an otherwise good servant. The poorer the man, the more highly he values his honour; it's all that he has. You touch it, and he will be compelled to go away.

When you hire a servant ask him whether his family is coming to live with him in your servant quarters; if so, find out how many children there are. It is no problem for him to live with six or eight others in one room but it's you who may not fancy having children's shouts and cries and women's chatter just round the corner the whole day long.

When a servant has stayed with an expatriate family for many years, he is entitled to their generosity. Some expatriates express this in form of a trust to help his son study, others open and fund a bank account for him or buy him a small piece of agricultural land, or a buffalo. A servant is normally also grateful though mostly he does not show it for used clothes in good condition. In between, traditionally twice a year, mostly at Eid and Christmas, he gets a new piece of cloth for a new shalwar kamis suit. This is important.

Women are mostly good ayahs but have rarely been trained as household servants.

For parties, neighbours and expatriate friends lend the services of their cooks. All servants get a special allowance or tip for late night services.

Unwanted Surprises

When the bell rings let the servant open the door. Instruct him not to admit any stranger. He should report to you and you make the decision. Quite often, your bell rings and you find a young person, a child or a bearded man standing at the gate with an official looking book or notebook in his hands. They want donations for various purposes: orphans, mosques, refugees, widows, students and what not.

The utmost caution is necessary as many of these are fake. Few people donate either to government welfare agencies, NGO's (non-government aid agencies) or private persons. You don't hear of results and too much has disappeared in wrong pockets. There are some organisations, though, where you may donate fearlessly and people do so, even with enthusiasm and anonymously as they have proved their worth.

Of late, criminals have been appearing at the door who introduce themselves as having been called to repair the TV, air-conditioning or whatever. Your servant should let them wait outside till you are back home, or else you might find your house empty when you return from a shopping spree. Obviously though, if you are expecting Pakistani or other friends, it would be rude to make them wait outside the door. Tell the servant when or whom you expect so that he can admit persons of your social circle.

Pets and Other Animals

Dogs are a good deterrent for unwanted visitors, preferably those breeds which look large and bark loudly. At night, keep the dog inside the house or chained near the door so that no ill-intentioned person can throw poisoned meat near him. All pets should be inoculated regularly, mainly against tetanus and rabies. There are plenty of stray dogs which generally look diseased. If your pet is a bitch it's better to have her sterilized or kept indoors, as it's virtually impossible to keep these strays out.

Some foreigners have adopted a stray puppy to keep and rear, only to find after a few months of good keep and food, that something the size of a wolf is standing before them. Mostly, these dogs have to be put to sleep when the expatriate departs.

If you want to shoo away some of the quite frightening looking hordes of stray dogs, just pick up a pebble and pretend to be throwing it. Even the pose of bending will send these hordes to flight. Long haired dogs brought from colder climes often suffer very badly during summer, and need to be kept in air-conditioned rooms in order to avoid heat stroke.

The favourite pet is the cat. It enjoys a privileged position as it plays a certain role in the Islamic mystical tradition. Birds or fish are rarely kept. In the face of great poverty and human suffering, not many emotions are left to be spent on animals. Apart from considerations of utility, the Pakistani has a much stronger affinity to the water buffalo than to indoor pets.

Beware!

There are two dangerous animals all over the country; the snake and the scorpion. The biggest snake is the stately cobra. Some species are not poisonous but when one comes sneaking towards you, you are hardly likely to know which kind it is. When venturing out, whether in the countryside or town, wise people carry a cane or walking stick. They say that a snake's attention can be diverted by a stone-throw, and a quick and strong hit with the stick will rid you of the danger. Snakes have often been found hanging right down from the doors inside old houses. Still, this is rare, and the snake has by and large fled from crowded cities.

The yellow and the black scorpion, both occur in Pakistan. The yellow type is more deadly. Scorpions are on the decline in cities and apartment blocks, but in an old bungalow in a large cantonment garden, you may find a scorpion sitting in one of your bedroom slippers just as you are about to step into them one morning! Houses that have not been lived in for some weeks should be thoroughly cleaned and examined when you move in. In an empty house in a hill station, I have seen scorpions fall from the ceiling and sit on door knobs.

If you are stung by a scorpion or bitten by a snake, immediately press off the blood stream from the major vein (get help to tie a string around it) and rush to the nearest medical centre. Most hospitals have anti-serum ready in stock.

Summer Specialities

There are plenty of other annoyances, mostly during summer. The swarms of flies and mosquitoes for example. There, you have to be extremely careful with food items and water. Wash, sterilize, cover up, and eat soon after cooking. Modern mosquito repellants are quite effective, whether electrical or chemical. But one single mosquito left over in the dark of the bedroom or caught inside the mosquito net can cause a wakeful night.

Your household, like all others, will most probably also be afflicted by cockroaches, ants and silver-fish. The hardest of sprays and a nightly mix of boiling water with some spoonfuls of washing soda down the drains will relieve you of cockroaches — temporarily. Since the Creator has made them in such a way that they are even resistant to radioactivity, you can be sure that they soon appear again on the domestic scene.

The ants are relatively harmless if you accept that the tiny thousands of them may, during a night, eat through your piece of cake that you forgot on the kitchen counter in the evening. Some of their species have the habit of feeding on carpets, always eating in a straight line. One fine morning, you may find your rug consisting of two pieces. Since their work starts from underneath you do not realise what has happened until they are through with the work.

The silver-fish eat holes into cotton dresses hanging in your bathroom or dressing room, and also eat the lacquer off paintings. Always keep some bushels of the leaves of the *drek* tree (which grows everywhere) in every room and replace them when they are dried up — then you won't have silver-fish problems.

A special feature of the tropics are the small lizards. You may watch them sticking to the verandah roof on a summer night and, like lightning, shoot forward into the insects that dance around the bulb. After that, you see them munch, crocodile-fashion. But their special sweet dish is curtains, silk lampshades and the sweet paint on pictures. To kill them is an extremely nasty experience. There is one effective local repellant: keep fresh, broken egg shells in decorative vases, on closets or wherever, mostly on curtain rods.

Your Wala

After some days in your new home you will find that you have a variety of *walas* around you: the *dudhwala*, the *achbarwala,* the *sabsi-* and *fruitwala*, the *mach'hliwala*... Wala means 'someone from' and implies a man. The words before wala mean milk, newspaper, vegetable and fruit, and fish respectively. When the meter-readers come, they are the *gaswala*, the *bijliwala*, the *paniwala*.

This expression is not limited to persons coming to your home. The bazaar is full of walas. The dudhwala needs some attention. There is no such thing as pure, fresh milk here. It is diluted in varying degrees and you pay accordingly. Still, you need to test, on and off, that the expensive milk that you buy for 8 or 10 rupees a kilo maintains its steady level of cream. Sometimes, it's not only the dudhwala who dilutes it, but others who handle the milk before it reaches you.

On Tuesdays and Wednesdays you can't go to your *goshtwala* because these are the two meatless days all over the country. In hotels, too, you only get chicken on these days. But in cities, there are shops with freezers just as in well-do-do homes. The freezers do not know of meatless days. Otherwise, it is observed by all.

There is the *ch'hatwala* who sells spicy hot or sour pickles. Almost anybody can become a wala. Servants who cannot use the sophisticated word *shaur* (husband) or are too shy to use it, turn you into a *gharwala*, a houseman, and your wife is the *gharwali*, the housewoman. Another wala is the *ru'i-safa-karnewala,* the cotton cleaning man. He goes from house to house announcing himself in a voice that resembles the whirring sound of his instrument which looks like a harp. He then squats before the heap of greyed, used cotton that the women of the house have taken out of the quilts, and moves the tense strings of his harp over the lumps of cotton in such a manner that they fly up and break into fluffy flakes while sand and dirt fall to the ground. This produces a guttural and rhythmic sound of trng-trng, trng-trng. Later, the women distribute the cleaned cotton over the washed cloth and stitch it again into a quilt. This always happens in autumn.

THE SUPPLIES
Electricity

All towns have electricity and about 60 per cent of the villages, too. There is only one nuclear power plant, near Karachi, while all other power is hydro-electric coming from three major sources: the gigantic Tarbela Dam, the world's largest earth-filled dam; the Mangla Dam; and the Warsak Dam, all at the foot of the mountains. Whenever there has been scanty rainfall the water shortage is felt acutely in form of load shedding which lasts for anything between 30 minutes to eight hours in a day. Every household keeps gas, spirit and other lamps ready.

The voltage is 220, but there are vast fluctuations between 160 and 250 volts. You need good stabilizers to protect your expensive electrical gadgets. There are two electrical systems: heavy duty power lines with three-pin plugs, and normal light lines with two, or the small three-pin, plugs. There are no standards and you need a variety of plugs to fit the many different kinds of sockets in the house. You will need twist-type bulbs to fit on to the local fittings.

Gas

Gas has come to the seven largest cities of the country during the seventies from a gas field in Baluchistan. It is earthgas and poisonous. There is a most important, life-saving rule concerning gas: never leave it on when you go out or sleep. There is no gas-shedding as such but the supply occasionally stops, and with it, the flame. When it comes on again, it streams out freely. Most winters there are some victims of such accidents, among them unwary foreigners.

Water

Water does not kill you but teases you in other ways. Water is always scarce — during some droughts it has even been sold by the bottle — and is supplied for about an hour a day; sometimes, not for days, depending on the locality in which you live. Where there is a concentration of foreigners the supply is more regular.

Every house has a large underground tank for storing supplied water. On the roof there is the overhead tank into which your pump pumps the water. Sometimes, the supply has not been enough; or the pump-belt broke; or the electricity goes off — whatever the reason, there you stand soaped and shivering and screaming for water under a dried-up shower. The answer is simple and always observed: keep a bucket of water ready in the bathroom.

Sometimes you will notice that the water level in the underground tank has gone down to alarming levels. Wise housewives then, instead of wasting precious liquid with tub-baths or showers, revert to the system that locals use and have used as long as memory goes: the *balti*-bath.

You take a large plastic mug filled with water from the bucket

and throw it over yourself. Then you soap yourself. After that, it's your decision how many mugs full of water you will use to rinse yourself. 2 mugs will take the soap off an experienced bather. With 10 mugs you feel like a king and deliciously refreshed. And you will be surprised to see that even then there is still nearly half a bucketful of water left. It's pleasure and economy in one.

The Mistri

You are often in for a rough time when something goes wrong and you need a workman, be it a plumber or electrician or another type. Such workmen normally do come the same day or, if you are extremely lucky, at the precise hour of their appointment.

After he has examined the defective item, the *mistri* will pre-scribe certain spare parts. If you let him buy them you can be sure that he will present you with a highly inflated bill. You either contract a workman from a shop that sells items related to his skill in the first place; or you begin a hunt for the spare parts. Some are very easy to get, but for others you have to travel to a distant specialised bazaar. Once you have all the parts together you once again begin to ring up and attract his attention to your problem.

One of your household, usually the servant, will have to watch over him or the defective part may just be plastered up or replaced by another second-hand, repaired spare part while your new one might disappear in the pocket of the mistri. He will also need your servant as an assistant (if he brings one along, it will reflect in the bill). It is wiser to have a man come to your house if an electric or electronic gadget needs attention rather than send the gadget to a repair shop.

Occasionally, you need a mistri or a gang of workers for a longer time for changes, additions to the house, paintwork, etc. Initially you will be pleased with the brisk spate of work, but by the second weekend at the latest, no mistri is visible. The worker is used to take his weekly wages home and will then remain with his family till the money is used up. Then he happily arranges with the village grocer to supply food to his family on loan and returns to work, though possibly not to your work. By now, the contractor will have found other jobs to do where he needs his workforce to prove his effi-ciency for a week or so. If there is no third party interested in his services, you will be lucky to have the mistri back after one week, or else after two, or three or who knows. Since the contractor relies on his agreement with you, you have to come down with a heavy fist. No contractor has yet stuck to his agreed time limit.

INOCULATIONS

Pakistan, apart from localized and seasonal outbreaks of cholera, is free from serious epidemics. Even the persistent smallpox has almost totally disappeared.

Occasionally you hear of typhoid; more frequently of malaria. You cannot fight all the mosquitoes around you all the time, so take the quinine tablets that the doctor prescribed you before leaving. All brands are available in Pakistan too. The vulnerable season is autumn and some foreigners restrict their quinine prophylaxis to this time of the year.

You can get all the latest types of vaccines. Typhoid inoculations are recommended and sometimes cholera. You can also have your children inoculated against whooping cough and measles in every city. Polio is hardly known in the Sub-continent but you can get the drops or vaccine without difficulty. Hepatitis vaccines are controversial and must be discussed with your doctor or the Tropical Medicine Institute of your country before you leave. Short term visitors might prefer to have them.

There is no yellow fever. Tetanus injections are given to injured persons immediately where the doctor might have a slight suspicion; or just as a precaution. TB is widespread but would hardly get near you — though do avoid sharing a communal hookah (see page 79). If you want to make really sure, have your servant screened. There is leprosy, mostly in slum areas. It is transmitted only after prolonged contact, so a leprous beggar poses no danger to you.

The Punkah

The *punkah* is a fan. There are the simple hand-held ones, made of reeds, which every villager can afford and which are also used to kindle the cooking fire. There are also ethnic ones and elegant ones. Then there are the 'imperial' ones now scarcely seen, where a servant sits on a verandah and moves a thick string up and down, throughout the night. The string that runs through a hole over the door and into the room moves a thick cloth on a frame over the sleeper and creates a mild breeze.

There are, of course, small table and wall fans, but they are child's play in Pakistan's hot temperatures. Every room therefore has one or two ceiling fans. Each of the three blades is some 50 centimetres long. Some foreigners are addicted to air-conditioners and can't stand punkahs. For others who cannot stand air-conditioners, punkahs are the only means of surviving the dreadfully hot nights. Whichever method you choose becomes irrelevant when your electricity supply goes off. And you can be sure that it goes off — more than you would wish.

WHAT TO DO IN THE EVENING

Most people here are starved of entertainment. Since the television came to the country in the mid sixties, people have forgotten to tell stories. The state (via the TV and the entertainment industry) is supposed to keep you busy in the evening.

Mostly people keep their TV set on throughout transmission time. When you visit friends, you will be lucky if they turn down the volume. Not that there is really much to see on the screen — but there might be just a bit of fun between the speeches and who wants to miss that? Most time is given to speeches; it is often no more than a permanent background drone. Mullahs speak at such length that people joke that they can see a mullah's beard grow out of the screen during his speech. The highlights are the English language films and series, and a few good Urdu films, mostly series of socio-critical nature. Well-to-do households have video recorders too, and in every bazaar there are video-film shops in plenty.

For bridge players, there are good bridge clubs and groups. You can establish contact with them through your city's 'Club'. The quiet family may take to reading, but most magazines are in Urdu. Pakistan's best *Newsweek* kind of magazine is called *Newsline*. It makes interesting reading. There are five major English language dailies that come out from different cities simultaneously: *Dawn* is the paper of Karachi; *The Nation* the one of Lahore; *The Muslim* of Islamabad; the *Frontier Post* of Peshawar; while the *Pakistan Times* is supra-regional.

In cities, socialising is the major evening activity. You can 'drop in' usually for a chat with a neighbour or friend. This trend is dying out in the 'modern' cities, where people of social standing are not available as they are too heavily booked with parties, receptions and dinners. Mostly, people send printed, formal invitation cards for these. Whether it is reading, bridge or socialising, all activities suffer quite often from one constraint: load shedding.

Load Shedding

When rainfall is scarce and water levels are low, the country suffers from electrical power shortage. This usually happens during winter but also in the pre-monsoon heat. The Power Authority announces the load-shedding timings in the Press but does not really stick to them. You find it out by experience. But it is really difficult at a dinner party when the hostess is just filling a bowl with soup for her guests and all are suddenly wrapped in darkness.

People have fixed gas lamps in various rooms; candles and torches help; the new portable, neon-light rechargeable lamp overcomes the worst. In Islamabad, load shedding is restricted to one hour four or five times a day, but in other cities (except Karachi) and in towns it is often many hours on end several times a day. Students and industries are the worst affected. In winter, people use the time for their evening walk; but in summer the only remedy is to be active, moving about to feel a bit of air or to 'sweat it out' in an attitude of acceptance of the powers that be or not be.

SCHOOLS

If you have children of school age, it is advisable to consult with other experienced expatriates in order to establish which schools are worth contacting, since there is a great difference in standards between the best and the worst private schools. Cities like Karachi, Lahore and Islamabad have the 'International School' which is recognised in US education circles. Some large missions have their own schools.

The best among the private or semi-private schools are the convents or other old missionary establishments which are run by the sisters and have qualified staff. In the private schools, the medium of instruction is English. The expatriate child will, however, be handicapped when it comes to subjects like Urdu, Islamic and Pakistan Studies. Several of the private schools prepare the children for 'O' and 'A' levels.

All school and college students wear uniforms. The approach to education is formal, and the standard of knowledge is quite good. But there is neither an effort to turn knowledge into thinking nor into development of character and personality. Youngsters, when they leave school or college, behave rather immaturely.

Higher Educational Institutions

There are some excellent colleges in the country, mostly those founded by missionaries. The medium of instruction is English. Numerous universities have sprung up and there are far too many, considering the country's negligible requirements for graduates. Doctors and engineers, ten years ago the dream of every young man and father, roam about jobless and stage demonstrations. Examination practices are often corrupt and the degree holds little value in the international market. Teachers are underpaid, research is neglected. The brain drain is a typical and sad outcome of the failure of the education system.

PLACES TO EAT

Pakistani cooking is delicious, with or without chillies or peppers. And since Pakistanis are hearty eaters, you find no dearth of restaurants and eating places in the cities and towns.

We shall skip the five-star hotels, which are like anywhere in the world. You can also get western style food in well established restaurants, where the menu card always shows sections of Pakistani, western and Chinese cuisine. Although they are expensive, Chinese restaurants are very popular. They have a touch of the foreign with their far-eastern decor and the Chinese ladies who generally manage the establishments. Pakistani families, particularly women, feel comfortable there. The food is also considered light compared to Pakistani food.

You must train your stomach to fight with oil and spices if you want to eat Pakistani style and not suffer afterwards. All food is good, tasty, clean and fresh, service is sometimes a bit clumsy, but always polite and attentive and the decor pleasant. Lahore especially abounds in eating places as the Punjabi is known for his solid appetite. Cheaper and smaller eating establishments should be visited only by those whose stomachs are germ-resistant, since these kitchens do not pass standard hygiene tests. You find very delicious snacks — hot, sour, spicy, sweet, very sweet — on carts at every street corner. A cautious expatriate leaves them alone.

A foreigner will get cutlery even if he has ordered Pakistani food. You might like to try to eat the local way: tear off a small chunk from your roti, form it between the fingers of your right hand into a small, open container and dip it into the curry on your plate. If you have ordered rice instead or in addition to roti, use three fingers to form a ball from a bit of it which is already soaked in curry. Then take it to your mouth without dropping a grain!

With the meal go fresh juices or bottled drinks. If you want plain water in friends' homes or 4- and 5-star hotels, you can be sure that it is boiled. Recently, factory bottled water has entered the market.

After the meal, coffee or a delicious cup of flavoured green tea is due. It is common practice to tip the waiter for his polite attention shown you. The tip is in accordance with the size of your order.

For more detail of the types of food available, see Chapter 6 page 102.

THE MEDICAL INSTITUTIONS

It is said that in Pakistan, you can do anything and get away with it; but do not fall sick!

The Government Hospitals

These institutions are similar to those in the education sector: although basically well equipped, they suffer from overcrowding. There are some new modern hospitals alongside old ones. But all have their modern X-ray departments, sections for different diseases, latest operating theatres with modern equipment, free medicine stores and treatment rooms. Some have the latest radiology, dialysis and other such facilities. Doctors are highly qualified and very often from abroad; there are nurses in plenty, and beds and food are quite good. And yet, nobody who can afford private treatment will go near a government hospital.

There, you register first and get a number. This is very important. They won't even let you die there without a number. After that, you ask your way to, say, the dental department. When you have found it at the end of the crowded passages, you sit along with other co-sufferers on wooden benches till your number is called, and you are called and examined.

In-Patients

In the old type or township 'private first-class' room in a government hospital, you generally have two rooms, a verandah, a courtyard and a bathroom. You take your own bedlinen and food and bring an attendant with you who cooks for you or brings the food, washes you and the linen, changes your sheets, buys the medicines that the doctor prescribes for you, brings the gossip from the neighbouring attendants and sleeps there on a mattress from home.

Doctors are highly qualified and skilled. The diagnoses are correct and most complex surgery is done just like the best in England or USA. It is quite a ritual to be sick and more so, in a hospital. The sick person is never allowed to be left alone, in case it looks as if he does not belong anywhere. Therefore, while you struggle with the after-effects of the anaesthetic, whole clans of people arrive and squat around the bed the whole day long. Nurses like it because the patient is now fully taken care of. Entertainment-starved villagers find it an interesting outing.

The corridors of hospitals look like passages of mass migrations. No wonder that their hygienic standards suffer and accidents happen. Doctors often look after a government hospital department in the morning and after their private clinic in the evening.

The Private Hospitals

Cities abound in private hospitals and towns, too, have some, but there are virtually none in the rural areas. Moneyed people live in cities — or travel there when they are sick.

In private hospitals, you find quiet, cleanliness and discipline. Doctors are sensitive and diagnose accurately. There are three disadvantages though: private hospitals often do not have the sophisticated equipment that government hospitals, or military hospitals, have. Also, doctors prescribe antibiotics too easily, even for a cold. And lastly, no doctor keeps a record: when you come again, how can the doctor remember the names of the medicines that you took the last time! Therefore, most expatriates prefer to go abroad for major medical problems.

There is no health insurance in the country yet. Government servants get reimbursements and some large companies repay a certain percentage of the medical expenses. The government has long been working on a comprehensive system of health cover.

In the cities, you find excellent dentists with the latest equipment and technology. The dentists are highly skilled and have very modern equipment. There are families who, after leaving Pakistan come here on a holiday mainly to have their ailing teeth treated by their old dentist.

SOCIAL AND WELFARE ORGANISATIONS

These institutions are run either by the government or privately. Expatriates take an active part in their activities. Most of them are concerned with the improvement of women, the education of children, and the care of the destitute, the sick and the handicapped.

Foreign wives mostly join women's groups who once a week meet to stitch, embroider, knit, paint, model, shape, cut and sew with the view to, once a year, selling their products at *meena* bazaars. These are most colourful fairs enriched by the flavours of innumerable local and foreign dishes and cakes.

There, for once, women dominate. Every city has these fairs. Missionary groups hold their fair before Christmas which is always an added attraction for every Pakistani. It is amazing what a variety of skills get pooled and what artistic and imaginative items are produced. The profits then go to hospitals, orphanages, schools, women's centres, welfare centres and the like.

Occasionally, foreign women go to such centres, schools or slums to render direct and practical help, to teach and heal. It is generally expected that women show an attitude of concern for their domestic servants who all belong to the poor. While an air of authority is always recommended, the expatriate wife might like to teach the servant's child the alphabet or bear the school expenses and assist financially in case of sickness in the servant's family. Used clothes in good condition and those no longer needed are automatically given to servants and, in between, a length of new shalwar kamis material.

Beggars

Most Muslims give alms either as routine or from religious motives. Most of them and almost all shopkeepers keep single rupee notes ready. There are several categories of beggar. The largest contingent are the professional beggars.

The professional beggars are loud-voiced and demanding, with woeful tales, who push their babies and children towards you, or expose their ailments. They are organised by their bosses and placed at strategic points in connivance with the police who, for a ten rupee note, do not notice them. Many of them are quite well-off, some have even become millionaires. But, since begging is profitable they continue to live and beg in dirty and torn clothes and with unkempt hair.

Another group are the casual beggars. They are men, women or children with low incomes. They might be sitting in the bazaar for a chat or on an errand. Upon seeing a prospective donor, they rush at you with the professional beggar's voice. If you refuse, they turn back abruptly to what they were doing.

There are religious beggars, holy men from many groups and shrines. You recognise them by their bead necklaces and long robes and long, unkempt hair. The mystic is not supposed to follow secular pursuits. Hence, he lives from alms.

There are innumerable children who, knowing that people tell them to work rather than beg, offer to wash your car. They are turned into professionals by poor and illiterate parents.

Then, there are the 'private' beggars: very old men and women, hardly able to move, with no relatives to care for them, who are genuinely in need of your money and concern. If you have a few notes ready when you pass such beggars, they will be gratefully received.

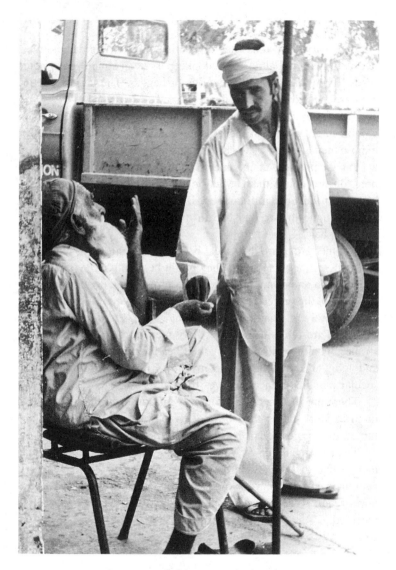

A young truck driver stops to give alms.

YOUR MAIL

By and large the postal system is a reasonably reliable institution, provided you know about and apply certain basic rules.

Letters

Your letters should not be too thick or people may think that they contain something interesting or profitable. Glue letters carefully. Put your rubber stamp or name label or one of the stamps where the four folded lines meet at the back of the envelope. Don't fix philatelic stamps on the envelope and then drop it in the box. Also tell your correspondents to avoid doing so. Have all mail except normal local letters stamped in front of your eyes at the post office. Central post offices have a special counter for it. Photo postcards with a beautiful scene or pretty face might not attract you only! It's best to put them in envelopes.

Airmail letters generally reach the addressee within the expected normal time. Registered letters are safer than normal ones. If one should get lost there is no point trying to trace it, and you may waste a lot of time over it. Make sure you get your magazines and books under registered mail, as they might contain pictures which are of burning interest and would also sell very well in the market. The delivery man has often been found to be a defaulter. To avoid such problems people give them handsome tips at Eid and Christmas. Alternatively, open a post office box. Pakistan issues plenty of beautiful philatelic stamps. Central post offices have a special section for their display and sale.

Parcels

A parcel is not accepted by a post office unless it is stitched in cloth and sealed with sealing wax.

Overseas parcels go through a customs procedure which is cumbersome. You need to be well aware what items are permitted to be imported and which are subject to customs duty and at what

149

rate, or the gift parcel on your birthday might turn out to be a very costly affair for you. For parcels over one kilogram you will be called to the central post office to attend the 'opening ceremony' and evaluation.

Telegrams

You can send domestic or international telegrams from a telegraph office or through the phonogram service. The telegrams do not always reach the addressee with either method.

In recent years, private mailing companies have become an established and reliable method of fast forwarding and delivery of all kinds of mail. You just call up and the consignment will be collected. You need to show them the contents of the despatch before sealing it. Monetary notes are not accepted for despatch.

Bills

Between your letters in your box you will find blue or green framed computerised sheets which will soon become an object of dislike for you. They are your bills: electricity, gas, water and telephone, and are generally very high.

These often arrive on the last date before payment becomes overdue, and generally have to be paid at one particular individual bank. If you can spare your servant or office boy for a few hours, do send him there; the queues there are very long, and most people hold handfuls of bills! Ladies fare better: they form a different queue which is much shorter and usually inside the bank building.

TRAVELLING

There are three means of travel within the country: rail, air and road.

The Railways

Thanks to British Colonial rule the country has an extensive railway system, yet overland travel nowadays is a rather less luxurious undertaking. You need to queue up for a ticket in any class, air-conditioned, first or second, two weeks in advance the moment the counter opens; and trains are not often on time. They are extremely crowded and journeys are lengthy. From Peshawar to Karachi takes you 36 hours. Food is poor; most people carry their own hotbox and thermoses for water. Whoever can, has friends or relatives standing at various railway stations who hand them fresh food and water into the compartment.

Ladies travel in different compartments or sections, but in the air-conditioned class full families may travel together. If you can stand it and want to see most of the land and people while travelling, the train is your choice. People often prefer the train for shorter trips of six hours or so between Lahore and Rawalpindi and Rawalpindi and Peshawar as it is safer than road travel.

Pakistan International Airlines

PIA, the national airliner, has a modern fleet of different aircraft, highly qualified and skilled pilots, polite cabin staff and can compete with many of the world's airlines and come out ahead. The

151

domestic flights are so heavily booked that you need to buy your ticket well in advance.

Travel Agents

Cities abound in travel agents, but few are registered or IATA members. Some may sell you tickets on a flight which is overbooked. Foreigners therefore normally book their travels with the reliable WALJI company that has branches in all cities. They also lead in organised group travel to mountains for walking, trekking and climbing and for sightseeing to cities and sites in their own, clean fleet of air-conditioned buses. Horizon Travels caters in a unique way for treks and hikes to the most outstanding feature of the country: the mountain world. If you prefer to travel alone you can hire a self- or chauffeur-driven limousine from them.

Public Transport

The public transport system is an experience in itself. From merrily smoking and roaring buses to clip-clopping tongas, it is for you to choose. Most foreigners enjoy a tonga ride: choose a public holiday with less traffic for a more comfortable tonga experience. And enjoy the open air, even if it's full of dust.

If you choose a bus, you may have another story to tell. It's like first aid after drowning — mouth to mouth breathing. You are lucky if you can take the ride on the baggage carrier on top of the bus because of over-crowding inside. You only inhale the normal pollution from which every big city of Pakistan suffers. Auto rickshaws have developed their own particular danger: the passenger cabin has an iron bar just above your head which hits it every time you go over a pothole or other such road feature.

Except for the buses, all other modes of transport should be bargained for. The fare meter dutifully displayed in taxis is only for the benefit of the police. Always agree upon the fare before you get in. At Karachi airport you will find outside the International Arrival

Some traffic participants in a small town.

Hall a policeman who registers the taxi that you want to use and gives you his own telephone number; it forces the taxi driver to charge the meter rate. A good and honest driver deserves a tip. In Lahore, the government recently introduced the 'Yellow Cab Service'. These taxis go by the meter and are considered a relief from the taxi driver monopoly. The cars are new and don't break down in the middle of a trip.

Islamabad is a new city and therefore, an exception. Here, roads have better signs, traffic volume is less and there are hardly any backways.

Road Transport

Road travel, whether by car, wagon or bus, is extremely alarming to the foreigner. The buses and wagons race each other three abreast

153

on blind turns to collect waving passengers before the others can pick them up. The more passengers a driver has, and the more trips he can make, the more the driver gets paid. They, therefore, travel distances in a day that western labour laws would consider criminal. To keep themselves awake, they take *charas*, a mild kind of marijuana.

Pakistan has one of the highest accident rates in the world. The short buses, or Flying Coaches, are air-conditioned and have more comfortable seats. They start a journey whenever they are full, which is generally fairly quickly. Bus stop signs are not easily recognisable. Look out for a cluster of people on the roadside. That's most likely the spot where you get on the bus — if you can. The gaily painted private transporters, however, are ready to pick you up from wherever you signal to them if no policeman is around.

Inter-town and inter-village roads are narrow and there, the race takes on different forms. The oncoming bus feels superior to your small car and insists you go off the tarmac. You might signal to him that, what with your small tyres, it is difficult to turn down into the dust or mud 15 centimetres deep at the side of the cracked and broken tarmac while he, with his huge wheels and strong shock absorbers, can do it easily. It is a matter of better nerves. Either you, philosophically, take the plunge; or, you continue straight at him — and he at you. Most of the time you lose. He has more experience and better conditioned nerves than you.

There are some chivalrous drivers though: they go off the tarmac while still at a distance to show you that you may continue straight. You can't help but deeply appreciate the gesture. Make sure you express it to them by a wave of the hand or by flashing your lights.

Which Car to Buy?

All models of Japanese cars ply the roads of Pakistan. Spare parts are easily available as well as trained mechanics. Workmen manage to put the oldest engines and heavily smashed bodies back on the road — they are wizards at it! Apart from Japanese cars, you see Morris Minors of the fifties plying as taxies, the last Volkswagens of the same vintage as well as Opels, some French and other European makes.

If you do not enjoy diplomatic privileges the purchase of a car here is expensive. As a diplomat, you will be allowed one car free of customs duty as a household allowance. Import tax starts at 100 per cent and goes up to 300 per cent or more. On top of it come a 15 per cent sales tax and some other minor taxes.

There is compulsory car insurance, and full cover insurance. But

155

you still need experience or a good lawyer to get your claim accepted. All kinds of petrol and diesel are easily available at convenient distances.

The 'Volkswagen of the people' is the locally assembled 800cc Suzuki car. You have to book one several months in advance. The prestige cars are Pajero, Mercedes and BMW. You could build a 5-room house with the money that one of these cars costs. Many foreigners keep a jeep or other tough vehicle for adventurous drives through the rugged countryside as well as a city car.

Road Hazards and Highway Chivalry

There are not many road signs. Some of them are in Urdu, some in English. Many roads carry two names, one that they had before partition and the other that they got after partition. The modern names are of people who were active in bringing about partition, e.g. Chundrigar Road replaces MacLeod Road and so on. Most city dwellers know them by both their names.

When driving in Pakistan, don't rely on any other road user to do what you would expect. If the car in front of you is indicating left, he may turn left, he may be warning you not to overtake, or he may simply have forgotten to switch the indicator off. In towns, people with trays frequently display their goods out on the streets. Road surfaces are unpredictable, with potholes and occasional floods; road signs are erratic and generally in Urdu; traffic lights do often exist, yet accidents happen as, sometimes instead of yellow, no light shows at all and drivers think they are switched off or broken. As well as cars, road users include donkey carts, camels, rickshaws and bicycles, who generally pay no heed to traffic signals. Night driving, where only a small proportion of road users have lights and those that do dazzle you, is strictly for the foolhardy and is best avoided.

Parking is only a problem in Lahore and Karachi, where cars are towed away. Try to find a spot where others have parked and place your vehicle in the middle, so the traffic police will reach it last.

Avoid offering lifts to strangers as this can cause complications; they would not expect a foreigner to stop. A male driver should never offer a lift to an unaccompanied woman, though a woman driver could pick up a stranded school- or college- girl.

Always keep your driving licence and car registration papers with you or, at least, a photocopy of them. Though foreigners are hardly ever stopped and checked by police, you will need them if you unluckily get involved in an accident. If you are a witness to an accident try to avoid being registered as such if possible. Normally, the heirs of your grandchildren will still be going to court over it!

If you yourself are involved in an accident, look out for a policeman or an educated looking local and place yourself under his protection. Very quickly masses will assemble and the foreigner is rightly or wrongly labelled the guilty party. You need the intervention of an enlightened local or the authority of police to calm down the masses and assure them that justice will take its course. The police often recommend you to leave the spot without waiting for a second and report the matter from your home telephone. It needs quick and judicious understanding of the situation to know what to do. At any cost you must avoid accumulation of and confrontation with large numbers of people.

As a traffic participant, never lose your temper. The two Suzuki drivers who stand side by side and block the road are just old friends who met accidentally and enjoy a little chat. What is even worse for weak nerves is that they will yield to your protesting honks or shouts only reluctantly and with an air that says: you are rude to disturb us thus!

PLANNING A TRIP?

For a weekend out you can use any means of road transport on all the major roads,which are reasonably good and wide. Speed, though, is somewhat slow. There are many old vehicles that you need to

overtake if you go in your own car; often, army convoys too, which take great patience; buses, that refuse to let you pass; there are tractors and tongas creeping at 10 kilometres per hour, crowds waving and stopping buses.

Directions and distances are frequently and well marked. Filling stations for petrol and diesel are at convenient distances. The road network is considerable. If you need to go on an unpaved road you are then in an area where you need a local with you. Not that there is any danger but you need to find the right track, and to be able to communicate with villagers, find help, water, guidance, fix a problem and so on.

Maps are quite accurate but not really detailed. For any direction beyond the tarmac roads, you must depend on local advice. For maps, contact the Pakistan Tourism Corporation in every city or a large bookshop.

Overnight Out?

In the ten large cities and in the established hill stations you find hotels of all categories. When you prefer a 4-star hotel, the only spot you need to check on is the bathroom — if that is OK, you will be alright. If you are a member of your city's club you may avail yourself of their accommodation services in other cities. Before departure, you need to make a reservation and pick up an introductory card from your own club.

The rooms in the clubs answer the needs of the normal traveller: they are comfortable, air-conditioned in summer and heated in winter, with modern bathrooms, carpeted and with all the essential furniture. The important aspect is that they are much cheaper than hotels; the same goes for the meals there, too.

Resthouses

In places other than cities, hotels become a problem for most foreign travellers. There, they are very modest and often not so clean and mostly with only the eastern squat-toilet, and without cooling or heating. They lack modern comforts.

However, at many scenic spots and also in towns at certain distances, various government and semi-government organisations have their resthouses. Some are simple and neglected, others comfortable or outright luxurious. Mostly, they have at least two bedrooms with or without air-conditioners but with sheets and blankets, bathrooms with towels, a dining room with all crockery and a kitchen with all cooking utensils, a sitting room with sofas or even a television set, large gardens and a cook and other servants who prepare your meal and attend to your needs most happily. In some of them, you can spend a weekend in comfort and spacious luxury.

You can only get there by connections. If you want to stay in a forest resthouse in a hill station when all hotels are full, or at one of the luxurious resthouses of the Water and Power Development Authority at a barrage, or a site-rest-house at a dam, you need to know someone in the respective organisation who will give or send that slip of paper, upon which the resthouse servant will open the doors to you. Occasionally too, an expatriate who introduces himself through his company or other credentials is extended this courtesy. You can make the request a week or ten days before departure but

not earlier. The resthouses are meant for touring or inspecting officials and accommodation can be given to you only if it is known to
be available. Upon leaving the resthouse, you sign the register and
pay the indicated amount, which is nominal. Often, the cook there
knows the amount due. Do not forget to reward the staff for their
help during your stay.

Beach Huts

If you want to enjoy a day at Karachi's beautiful beach you will
need to have access to a beach hut or chalet. The beach is lined with
these two to three room cottages. Some are in dilapidated condition,
others are comfortable but all look drab and a bit run down from
outside. The violent monsoons and salty air there make the best
concrete crumble within a few years. Therefore, people pay little
attention to the looks of them. Inside, they contain all the basics for
sitting, resting and eating and each is guarded by a man paid for the
job. There is no electricity. Many Karachi companies own huts and
some private persons do, too.

Most expatriates have contacts with company officers who will
book the hut for them and give them the key. There is hardly ever
a fee, it's common courtesy. You pay the guard at the hut for
helping you, cleaning the hut and getting water for your tank. You
need to make sure that you leave the hut in the same condition as
you found it and lock it securely.

SPORTS

Most major sports are played in Pakistan. The whole country is
addicted to the game of cricket. From October to March is the
cricket season. Either at home, or abroad, cricket series are played.
This game of gone-by imperial days lasts three to five days; and
when a final is played on Pakistani soil with a Pakistani team in it,
the government declares the day a holiday! Wherever the venue of
the games is, the people will stay glued to their transistor radios and

better still, the TV set. Cricket is played in every street that is not the main boulevard; boys use anything, even old chairs as a wicket. It is the national game of the country and Pakistan can rightly be proud of its official team. Hockey and football are played in schools and on open grounds reserved for this purpose in the cities, but the standard of football is not good. Apart from that, volleyball, tennis and squash are popular. Pakistan is frequently world champion in squash.

Already, we have touched on the elitist games. Tennis and squash you can only play in clubs, where you have a swimming pool, too. Badminton and table tennis are played everywhere. Every big city has a golf course for people with a lot of time; and a race course, though betting is prohibited. The northern areas of Pakistan seem to have been the cradle of polo. Pakistan has good polo teams, mostly from the armed forces as they have the finest polo ponies. Expatriates, apart from playing in clubs, often join the local teams for practice and matches.

There is not much for ladies in the field of sports, but they can be enthusiastic spectators at matches. They can swim in the clubs at the prescribed ladies' hours in the morning, and also at the general members' times if they wish to without a problem, play badminton and table tennis at home or at friends' or at outings and picnics. Girls play badminton and table tennis in schools and colleges. That is about all. Traditionalists object to women participating in public sports. A few daring women brave them, but they are so few. Also, their wide shalwars and dupattas do not permit the best of development of fast and precise movements. The performance is therefore poor.

It's only city youths who can play organised games. The country boys work. Their potential does not reach the sports scene. But on holidays they enjoy their most popular village sports — cockfights, with lots of secret betting, too. Other traditional village games include *kabaddi,* a kind of wrestling, very popular in the Punjab;

161

guli danda , a favourite skill game with sticks; and *geethe* is a team skill game with stones and a ball followed by run and hit which is great fun.

Kite flying is perhaps most popular (see below, page 163). Marbles and a kind of hopscotch are played as in other countries. The Punjab boasts famous heavy wrestlers, another popular week-end entertainment.

Some excellent sports goods are made in Pakistan. World Cups and Olympic Games are widely played with footballs and hock-eysticks 'Made in Pakistan'.

SOME SPORTS FESTIVALS
Basant

This is not a Muslim festival but a traditional one of the Sub-continent and it heralds the advent of spring. In Pakistan, it is limited to the city of Lahore around the first of March. On this day, people gather on roof tops or open fields and participate in kite flying competitions. The kites range in size from small to over one metre large and are made in two varieties: the square kite, or the double bodied *toukal*. The kite string is coated with ground glass to cut the string of the opponent's kite. The opponent can be anyone or rather, everyone that is near your kite.

When someone's string has been cut a shout goes up from the winner and his many supporters, drums are beaten and trumpets are blown. Children and men run around in the streets trying to capture the cut kites but hardly ever succeed: in the melee, the paper kites get trampled and broken. Food is prepared and served on rooftops. The rule of the kite competition is that when two kites are engaged, no other person may interfere with his own kite till one or the other line is cut. This is strictly observed. The professional kite flyers use leather gloves to fly kites as the strings may cut the hand badly.

This activity goes on throughout the day, with screams and

shouts, the beating of drums and blowing of trumpets, cheer and laughter, and the sky is studded with kites of every colour. In the evening the kites are pulled down and everyone is exhausted and jubilant. The evening is almost as exciting: the day's victories and strategies are recounted endlessly and battle plans are made for the next year. On the following day, every electric pole, every tree and telephone and electricity line is laden with broken kites.

The Lahore Horse and Cattle Show

This festival is organised by the government of Punjab, and takes place in the Fortress Stadium of Lahore in spring. This show is spread over three days. Tent pegging, trick riding, dog racing, display of camels dancing, horses dancing, and folk dances are all a part of the show. The show starts from about mid morning and continues throughout the day for the three days. Livestock is proudly displayed by the owners who bring their animals from all over the province to be displayed in the festival. The best stock is given prizes. Some of the best breeds of cattle and buffaloes are found in the Punjab, and each animal is a major asset of the family.

This festival really gives an insight into the culture of the Punjab as it is all related to an agrarian society. You will feel the pride of the people as they noisily display their skills at horse riding, or training animals, or at just looking after their livestock.

THE COUNTRYSIDE

The economic, cultural and social differences between city and country-life are stark. The visitor to the country will come in contact with villagers on their weekend outings or on more extensive tours through the country. Therefore it is important to throw some light on the life in Pakistani villages.

Villages consist of a collection of flat or double storied houses with adjoining courtyards, enclosed within a wall and linked by narrow earthen lanes bordered by open drains. In an alternative arrangement, landowners may have their houses within their fields, so single houses are spread over wide areas.

Some 60 per cent of the villages are electrified, which has changed certain traditional life patterns. The farmer will no longer go to sleep at nightfall but watches TV instead. About 85 per cent of the country's population is illiterate. As most educational establishments are in cities and towns, literacy in villages may be no more than 5 per cent. To write an application to a bank for an agricultural loan means for most farmers a trip to the city.

Village life is hard and frugal, and the mishaps of fortune — whether floods, drought, the death of a son or a buffalo — are borne with a stoic acceptance of the will of God. Rural women work in the fields with their menfolk, and in addition prepare their food, keep house and endure numerous pregnancies. There is flourishing agricultural production, but this is not as yet matched by modern agricultural techniques or a sophisticated marketing network.

The tourist will find earthenware, basketware, sandals and embroidered slippers, cloths, mirrorwork, metalwork, wooden carvings — a wealth of cultural riches . Do take care to examine any article you buy carefully, as occasional shoddy goods are found. The highlights of rural life are weddings and the annual folk festival or *mela*.

The Village Wedding

There is little joy in village life. A wedding is eagerly awaited as the whole village is the guest of the bridal parties. Women, a few in gaudy silks, others in cottons but all in biting colour combinations, march together to the bride's or groom's home where at least 50 kg of rice is cooked for a pillau and a sweet yellow rice. That's all. But the day is spent with drums, singing and dancing and excited chatter which sustains them for many dull months to come. The men, all with their best turbans on their heads, assemble in the neighbour's courtyard but there the scene is sober. On this day, they all look like a Malik, Khan, a Chowdhry or Mian sahib and often titulate each other this way. Honour is the only asset of the poor man and being addressed thus makes him feel really good.

After ritual and feasting are over, the bride is taken to the groom's home in a *dolki*, a small wooden box in which she can sit with her knees pulled up, high on the back of a garlanded horse or camel, the Mercedes of the rural population. Traditions here hold faster than in cities, often from sheer economic constraint.

Colourful, racing buses take the people of the countryside from village to village. Where there is no road or motorised transport system, the two-wheeled horse-drawn tonga serves the purpose. It is a five seater but mostly holds families of about 15!

Mela Time!

The only other village fun is the mela, the annual folk festival when a modest merry-go-round and other swings and slides arrive along with entertainment and feasting booths.

Sometimes women bring their children there but always in large groups together and firmly wrapped in their burquah. But what with a few swings and whirls, watching a dancing bear and monkey, a few pennies spent on a game and a few sweets or salty snacks all drowned in oceans of music and voices, people return home as happy as children anywhere in the world.

WOMEN'S ORGANISATIONS

The International Women's Club in the four provincial capitals holds monthly meetings for which it invites guest speakers from the international world of culture and science, or a government official. The association is very popular with Pakistani women and also has many foreign ladies as members.

There are Foreign Wives' Clubs in Islamabad, Lahore and in Karachi. The one in Karachi seems to be the most active one in the social help that it renders to other foreign women and wives: it introduces them to the complexities of the environment, helps them in emergencies and introduces newcomers to a social circle.

CLUBS

The big cities all have their old, traditional clubs: the Peshawar Club, the Rawalpindi Club, the Lahore Gymkhana and so on. Mostly, these date back to British colonial days, but the large wood panelled smoking rooms with wide easy chairs and etchings of governors and so on, substantial libraries and British style dining halls have generally been modernised. With the introduction of prohibition in 1976, the bars, the last remnants of those legendary days, lost their appeal, too.

Nowadays, clubs provide the same services but in the relaxed Pakistani style. Families may enjoy a holiday buffet lunch there. Wedding and other receptions are frequently held at clubs. All clubs have now expanded sports facilities from tennis, badminton, table tennis and squash to golf, swimming and, often, riding.

SEX AND OTHER CLOSE CALLS

Prostitution is banned by the government in Pakistan, but the oldest profession still operates. Since there are no massage parlours, bars or night clubs, prostitues operate through their own established networks. One keeps reading about raids on various prostitution dens, but still they exist. They operate through bell boys, waiters, taxi drivers and receptionists. Here it would be proper to add a word of warning: watch out for the 'con' artist. He may promise you a ravishing beauty, take your money and disappear. If you really wish for the company, don't part with your money until the lady has come to your room!

Dancing Girls

The dancing girls of the Sub-continent held a very high position in the pre-British era. Young princes used to be sent to these women to be trained in social behaviour. They were kept by kings and princes. These girls dance and sing only. In all the old cities of Pakistan you will still find their abodes close to the forts of the city. In Lahore right next to the fort is the most famous red light district, *heera mandi*; literally translated it means the 'market of jewels'. In Multan, Hyderabad, and Peshawar also, these areas are in close proximity to the forts. Social history gives the reason for these areas being close to the forts: those courtesans who grew old or fell from favour with the kings were turned out from the forts. Having nowhere to go they settled close to these forts and to date their heirs are still living there. Most of these dancing girls have been kidnapped and sold into these markets. Here, they are trained to dance and sing. The pimps have such a stronghold on them that there is no way for them to escape. Most of them were brought here at such a tender age that they don't even know where they came from.

As evening falls, the lamps on their balconies light up, and the girls come and stand under the lights, trying to solicit customers, who are strolling about in the streets below. The customers come up to the room. The doors are closed, the customers sit on the carpeted floor with cushions to lean against. Cold drinks, tea, and pan are served to them. The musicians strike up the music, the dancer starts to sway with the beat, and another girl or girls sitting with the musicians will start to sing. The clients will shower money on the dancing girl, which will be collected from the floor after the song is finished. There are several ways in which this money is offered; it may be waved over the head of a friend from where the girl is supposed to collect it, or it may be placed on the cheek of a friend, and again the girl is supposed to take it from there while she pinches the cheek, at times drawing blood with her nails. This continues till the customers leave, or run out of money.

167

At some marriages, or on the birth of an offspring, these women are invited to come and perform at the houses of the well-to-do and landlords, to liven up the occasion and offer entertainment to the guests.

You may be a witness to this, and your host may give you some money to offer to the dancing girls. The way to do it would be to go over to your host and wave the money in a circular motion over his head and let the girl take it from your hand. This can be an extremely costly affair, so don't offer your own money. Plead ignorance to the ritual. What happens is that there is a deal that has been worked out between the host and the dancing girl. All the money that she collects will secretly be recirculated through the hands of the host while the other guests continue getting fleeced, till they stop. The host cannot run out of money. To do so would make him lose face among his friends.

Transvestites

These are perhaps the lowest and most pitiable group in Pakistan. Their existence is accepted as part of the social set-up but they are looked down upon, ridiculed, and generally treated with contempt. Their part in society is to find out where a son has been born or a marriage is taking place and to barge in singing a popular melody in off key, guttural voices. The crowd will listen to them for a while and then give them some money and get rid of them. Historically they used to serve the servants in the women's section of the kings' and princes' 'harems'. Nowadays, they are just a notch above beggars in the social circuit.

Chapter Nine

BUSINESS IN PAKISTAN

WORKING IN PAKISTAN

If you are with a multinational firm or international agency your job is more or less already known to you. There, the only unknown factors are your fellow workers and how to develop a working relationship with them.

A foreign colleague generally enjoys great respect. A foreigner's attitude of fair deal, fair treatment, efficiency and honesty are factors which are known and respected by almost everybody. In addition, you are a guest in the country — which is not just an empty phrase. You will be treated with great respect for this reason alone.

THE BUSINESS STRUCTURE

Most business establishments in Pakistan are owned and operated on a family basis. The final decision-making power is always vested in the eldest member of the family who is usually the father or the eldest brother. The reasons for this method of operating are twofold: firstly, the business has started and then expanded from there. But the deeper root is historical: relatives are the most trustworthy companions in business in a world that has been for centuries extremely competitive, poor and vulnerable to interference from overlords. In this way clans and castes have formed; and apart from honesty, the family-business clan can defend the common interest like no outsider.

Most businessmen and traders are usually not trained in business methods, yet they have a good business acumen. Business is preferably conducted among friends. A personal relationship guarantees a business relationship, too. For the same reason a whole family owns and runs a company. The profit span is therefore often less important than the knowledge of who is buying or selling a product.

Many large companies have modernised their establishments including the administration which is run quite on western lines. Even if professionals are engaged as managers, the controls will still be in the hands of the family.

PAKISTAN'S EXPECTATIONS

What is expected of you as a foreigner working in Pakistan?

1. You must be quick in recognising the authority of your superior and develop a good working and social relationship with him.
2. Make sure that you can present your figures with authority. For this, you need to be well informed about the country's laws, government regulations, trading methods, forms and formats.
3. It is often more important to have a social relationship in order to 'fit in'. You need to be a convincing conversationalist.

4. Do not act in a superior manner. It will ultimately turn against you and bring you problems. Once you get a 'label' in your office, word will spread quickly and will affect the flow of your work. Some cases are known where the foreigner had to leave as he could not elicit the required co-operation from fellow workers due to his bossy attitude.

5. Remember that in your working environment you are a guest even after many years. You can, with all politeness, capitalize on this position.

6. Unless they are in written form, the Pakistani boss will not issue orders. He will request his staff in polite words to do this or that and take time to explain unclear factors to them. Do likewise.

7. To say: 'This office is dirty' will earn you frowns. If, instead, you stimulate your staff's co-operation by asking for suggestions on how to improve the looks of the office you will probably get good results. In the end, it must be your decision or that of your counterpart or boss. You may still influence the spirit of the activities.

8. Knowing and using a few words of Urdu will help a lot.

The Transfer of Technology

You as a foreign expert are supposed to teach the local people your skills. Therefore, you must set an example by the way you work and conduct yourself. More than any words, the personal example is respected and followed in this patriarchal society.

Staff have normally a lot to tell each other. What, after all, is life for? You work all day, get low wages, pleasures are few, there's always some illness or other in the large family causing extra expenditure, then inflation... a huge packet of worries. A chat with equals helps, and makes it a shared burden then. All day, tongues are moving in competition with the teacups. The consultant or foreign partner must consider the importance of the relationships between the poorer sections of society before he pronounces his strict: 'DISCIPLINE PLEASE'. The handling of this type of situation must be considered a major decision.

Transfer of technology is, however, mostly understood in terms of machines and their handling. This is fraught with dangers and problems. A European or American has grown up 'together' with machines. The grandfathers handled the first, simple ones and the following generations were mentally prepared to absorb and handle greater sophistication. Machines are a part of the western environment. Figuratively speaking, every child knows how to handle a machine. But how many homes in Pakistan have a computer?

A machine is, for the Pakistani worker, an impressive, imposing, monstrous, challenging and above all, foreign entity; he has not grown up with it, the men and boys in his village did not discuss how to operate a slide projector, his mother did not switch on the washing machine...

The worker is now taught the handling, servicing and routine of his position on the production line. He enjoys doing it. It gives him a feeling of power and is a means of connecting him with the modern world. But often he has not really understood the requirements, the soul of the machine. You will understand what I mean when you see the simple taxi-driver creep behind slow traffic — in fourth gear! He has, as yet, no relationship with the sounds of the engine.

A golden rule is not to introduce any machines without training the staff abroad or, at least, in the same type of environment here. This is usually done. Yet, accidents still happen where the mind is not tuned to machines and sometimes cause disaster.

Certain international experts lobby for the supply and use of technical equipment for Pakistan produced not later than the 1950s. Such machinery is much simpler to handle, easy to service and stronger than more modern equipment, but this goes against the trend in the country which demands the latest technology. Many interpret their 'modernity' by the number of sophisticated machines around them. Where the westerner is quite happy with an older model of a musical instrument, here, the young man must have the latest, most sophisticated model and all extra gadgets with it. Even the craze for telephoning can be understood in this context. It is a point of controversy discussed at highest levels. Companies of course, make their own decisions.

Time Scales

The Urdu language uses the same word for yesterday and tomorrow: *Kal*! Now you know how important time is here. This concept is difficult for someone who has compartmentalized his life into time schedules. The ordinary Pakistani has no concept of time and he waits for events to happen and dictate to him the use of time. An important appointment can get delayed because an old friend came by to say 'hello!' When it rains, banks may open late because the clerks would get wet on the way. You will need a lot of strength to come down from your principles, training and better knowledge to be able to live with this attitude.

Meetings start with the usual cup of tea. Tea comes the moment you visit somebody in his office. You are a guest, even if you have gone to a colleague's office to clear up a point. And the cup of tea IS important.

Business is much better when discussed over tea. The atmosphere is more personal, which is important. The official is doing something for you, not for a purpose. It is much more satisfying to do something for a person than for a thing. But the officer needs to feel that you are a worthwhile and trustworthy object of his goodwill, co-operation and input, and that he can find out in his own style — over the cup of tea. Even if it takes a long time. The tea-boy, therefore, is the most important person in the office. If you claim that you have come to develop business and not develop friendship, you won't succeed in doing business.

173

How to Develop a Business Relationship

To do business you must be an insider first. What is meant is that you must get to know someone who will get you the right introductions. You need to identify the right person to act as your filter or confidant. But do remember that con men abound and you might be totally unaware of their existence. There is no malice meant in this but what it implies is that the average Pakistani cannot use the word 'No'. The reason for it is complex, it has a socio-political background. If you ask a favour and the person is unable to do it he will not say no, or sorry, but he will stammer that he will try. So you need some skill to find out who can really help you to get introduced to the right circles.

Another important thing to remember is that everything is spoken about in form of similes. Direct statements are seldom made unless the relationship is intimate or very old. Business is also frequently discussed in a roundabout way. You need to establish the credentials of character, loyalty and capability before matters are discussed with you in a frank manner and to the point.

Most family businesses maintain two sets of books, one for the authorities and the other for themselves. Most systems are corrupt. But even if you come to know of it, do not show that you know, and try to ignore it. It has its roots too deep in the system and you alone cannot reform anything. Bribery is common; so are under-invoicing, avoiding duties and taxes. The road-side traffic cop takes 'fees' and 'commissions' as willingly as those higher up the hierarchy. The number of cars that are seen on the roads and the number of villas compared with the average income of the people of the country gives some indication of how widespread corrupt business practice is. It is best that you do your work without getting involved in the other side of the business, or else some time later, you might run the risk of getting blackmailed about such dealings.

If you are married, your wife at some time or the other is going to get socially involved with your official life. Her behaviour is going to play an important role in the esteem and co-operation that you will receive. Remember that this is a rather closed society. It is best for you to be friendly but not jovial. Stories or comical situations of your married life that, elsewhere, might be a joke told in good faith and be received as such, might find a different sort of response here. A Pakistani colleague who is well educated and has been exposed to western life and countries will enjoy the joke — but would never tell one himself. 'This is how westerners behave,' he will think condescendingly.

If he really does tell such a joke or anecdote you may be sure that you have won his confidence. He tells it to show you that. For your wife it's best not to show emotions in public, as this is not done. She should be polite, friendly, benignly smiling, and yet natural.

The Pakistani Boss

The Pakistani boss who is running his own business does not come to office before 10 o'clock. I have known of a boss who used to enter his office at 2.30 p.m., and then work till midnight. He would expect his managers who came at 9 in the morning to stay at his beck and call till he had wound up his affairs and left for the night. This, however, was an extreme case. But the boss is the father figure in the office, an industrial continuation of the old landlord-peasant relationship with responsibilities toward his employees' families' welfare. Thus, lower staff expect from the boss a bonus on the marriage of their daughter or son, or when someone has died in the family. The boss, as the head, alone takes all decisions of that kind. He may consult his managers, but in all matters the final decision is his. A heavy duty of his is to maintain social and business contacts. A government official's son may find immediate employment because the boss of a commercial concern may need a favour from that official either now or at a future time. The growth and expansion of the business happen at the boss' discretion.

Among the staff you will always find some who have a special

175

relationship with the boss. These people may wield great power in a company. Try not to get involved in office politics which abound everywhere. All orders of the boss are to be obeyed, not questioned. He can make his people work on weekends or late if he wishes to.

The Personal Secretary

The clerical staff are of secondary social status. Often, they come from low income and low social background families where they enjoy the status of a *babu*, a man who can read and write. Their salaries are low and so are their skills. In recent times, the secretary who works on a computer has attained a kind of specialist status with higher social prestige and income.

Only large companies run on modern lines have a personal secretary to the boss, who is usually a woman trained to assist the boss, take certain decisions and carry certain responsibilities herself. Being educated, such a person enjoys prestige and respect in industrial cities where a totally new stratum of trained or specialist professionals has added to the breakdown of traditional concepts of class thinking.

Often, the personal secretary is a personal relation of the boss. He or she is then the invisible power in the company. You can be sure that all gossip reaches the boss within hours. Loyalty then also extends to the boss' personal life.

The Government Official

The government officials are vested with such powers that they wield great influence. They know that ministers and other officials of the government are like shooting stars in the sky, and that they are not there to stay. They transact all government procedures, in which there are so many legal loopholes that a dozen competent lawyers would come up with a dozen different interpretations of the law. If you want this to turn out in your favour you must know the expected 'fee' or 'commission' that is commensurate with the job to be done or the status of the official. Additionally, the personal assistants to government officials need your attention as all deals, granting of appointments and the like happen through them.

These P.A.s have normally survived many bosses and know procedures and affairs better than anybody else. They are an integral part of the system. And it is almost impossible to dismiss a government employee unless he has criminally defaulted. They all work together as a team in which everyone gets his due according to merit and status.

The Confidant

Unless it is a small matter you will need the help of the confidant to approach the official. Often it is the P.A., mostly a friend of the official. There, you need all your social and psychological skills, firm politeness, smiling readiness to compromise, a deep understanding of the undercurrents of a conversation, of a word spoken or not spoken, of a hint, and silence or a half smile — and you need to react quickly and as expected. He can make or unmake you. Talk to people who know him, around him, make discreet enquiries. Remember that the confidant makes his living on acting as the go-between. He will not do anything for nothing. But he will not name a price directly. This will be done in a roundabout way, maybe in the form of a neutral conversation in which the price of a certain item is mentioned. All fees and commissions will be taken by him to be passed on. The official never mentions these things personally; he may ask you to 'talk' to his confidant. Now you know what that means.

Resentments

There are innumerable aid agencies and company officials of foreign countries in Pakistan. All need government clearance before they can start their jobs. It is a known fact that these clearances take between months and years to happen; or, they may not happen.

177

Apart from the 'fees and commissions' issue there are other factors which are very often the cause of go-slows or withholding of official permission. It is a sensitive issue.

No doubt all foreign experts are highly qualified persons. That's why they are sent to developing countries. However, the government official is likewise a highly qualified and specialist person with often deeper knowledge and understanding. Yet, he struggles along on a government salary which is about ten times less than what a foreign specialist earns. He feels the pangs of injustice, for he feels qualified and is qualified to do precisely the same job that the foreigner does. On top of it, many foreign experts meet the official in a patronising manner, even if unconsciously.

And, over many years of experience, the Pakistani official begins to react psychologically: 'Why do these people come here, we know much better how to go about it, or, at least, we can do this job ourselves' and the like. Rational or irrational, he feels powerless, even vis-à-vis his own government system where he, as a Pakistani, would be an object of endless 'procedures' where the foreigner comes with a document showing international agreements. Many projects collapse because of such imponderable factors. The foreign expert or company official must heed what has been said beforehand: to establish a personal relationship with the official — the same goes for counterparts —, to gain his respect as a cultural entity, to give him the good feeling that you are on an equal footing with him in terms of rank and cultural background and that you understand his problems. Imagine a situation where you are a part of a system where you have to play with covered cards, with half-truths and ulterior motives; then, you come to sit opposite a person who with a smile opens all his cards before you, has a beneficial objective as a job and personal aim to offer you and all documents correct and complete. How would you react? Here, there is fear in many instances: these foreigners want to take more than they bring (think of 200 years of colonial past!), what could possibly be their real aim? Security problems due to the activities of the superpowers add to the fears. Before you come with any project make sure that you are not pressed for time. You have to allow things to move in the speed of the country.

Deadlines

Accept the fact that trying to get things done on time is something quite impossible. People do not recognise time pressures. Things will get done when they are fated to be done and nobody can change this. It will save your nerves and family happiness if you learn and accept this right from the start. You alone cannot change the system. You might wonder when at all anything gets done in this country. That is a million dollar question. The norm is to do the minimum work in the maximum time. But five minutes before the deadline the race begins: everyone works and runs around double speed and presents the results at the dot of twelve. The looks of it may not all please you. But everyone feels proud and satisfied with himself for this wonderful achievement.

Reschedules, time lapses or abandoned projects are common. Any sizeable project involves several strata of human beings. The businessmen, government officials and financing bosses each with their own requirements and psyches. Do not let any of them back out or the whole project will go into a tail spin. Do your bit patiently and firmly or you will be the one who ends up with ulcers or high blood pressure.

Bad News

Good news travels fast. Upwards, downwards and laterally. Bad news, on the other hand is hushed up and transmitted in private. No one is fired publicly. The affected person would lose face and, remember, honour is one of the most important issues in every Pakistani's life. So, no matter how aggrieved you are, keep your temper in check. Call the culprit into your office and reprimand him.

179

Always conduct such an interview in private.

If the bad news concerns you, you will feel it before it travels to you. People will either start avoiding you or will become over-friendly. But even the closest associate of yours in the office will not tell you the bad news. You have to take it all from the boss.

Decisions and the Boardroom

In the boardroom deals are discussed threadbare. You are an expert in your field. Provide your information and sit through the rest of the meeting and dream of golf or whatever. When the bargaining gets hot, tempers will flare, voices get loud and the language changes from English to Urdu. If the business is negotiated between two Pakistani companies a lot of inter-personal negotiations have already been conducted in a social setting before the question enters the boardroom. And right up until the signing of the document the search for a better deal will continue, and all contacts will remain open. If the company is family managed, the board sitting may be just a formality, and so will be your contribution. The eldest, the head of the concern, will make his decision with or without you though he will politely listen to your views.

In dealing with a government or foreign agency, a lot of lobbying has already been done. Friendships have been formed, old connections revived, relationships sounded, confidants started a flow of information well before the negotiations started. The board meeting then is only held to formalise the deal.

If you have come to present a project to a company in Pakistan with whom you have had no earlier association you can expect two kinds of reaction. It may be pursued hotly; or excuses may be offered, which means that another party has offered better 'fees'. You may react or leave it.

TYPES OF BUSINESS

There are two types of business in Pakistan: public limited and private limited companies. These follow the international principles of business and need no explanation. But most of the traders and businesses smaller in looks, but not necessarily in turnover are not even registered. All a Pakistani needs to start a business is a place, a telephone, stationery and contacts.

Therefore, before you enter into business with anyone — maybe even by correspondence — make very sure that the establishment exists with all legal formalities complete and is physically known to others in the trade. If your deal with someone is lucrative enough for him, a trader may then really get himself registered.

Businesses that only exist on paper often have the habit of changing their names once an authority such as the income tax appears on their doorstep or when you call to remind about payments.

Labour Laws

Workers in Pakistan are well protected through the labour laws and courts. Multinationals, private and public firms abide by the regulations. Unregistered firms though, do not often follow the law. There is abundance of underpaid woman-and-child-labour. Before Zulfikar Ali Bhutto in the seventies established the labour laws, hiring, firing and even physical maltreatment were common. Under the protection of the labour laws through trade unions, the labour force in the seventies retaliated with extreme severity, even beating up their managers. Now, it is almost impossible to dismiss a worker unless charges against him are serious. But the ethics and meaning of the unions are still largely misused. Under their umbrella the productivity of the country suffers. Workers have been told about their rights for political gains, but not about their responsibilities. Therefore, companies try to keep the head count of their workers as low as possible. In some companies, the labour force has now realised that they have to work in harmony with the management and vice versa. Managements by and large have recognised the human rights of the workers. The relationships mostly are not really easy but the situation is generally improving slowly.

You as a foreigner will hardly come face to face with labour problems. Also, your status as a guest in the country will keep you out of ugly situations. But never lose your temper. You can always plead ignorance about what they are saying.

OFFICE CONDUCT

Here are some tips on office etiquette:

1. In business life, a tie is customary and in winter a jacket. A tropical suit may be a better choice when you know that you have to visit an office that is not air-conditioned. It is very dressy and widely worn. For the Pakistani, the shalwar kamis, declared the national dress in the early 1970s, has become very popular and has widely replaced the western suit.

2. All meetings start and end with a handshake. When the boss, client or partner comes into your office, go around your desk to meet him and greet him warmly with a solid handshake. When he rises to leave, go to the door and accompany him out.

3. Do not come straight to the point. The weather, business conditions, the government and any latest news of the day should be discussed first. Learn to feel when the time is 'ripe' for starting the actual business.

4. Tea, coffee or cold drinks are offered as soon as your guests are seated comfortably.

5. Do not rush a meeting. If you have another urgent appointment you should not just say so. Instead, relate the background of your constraints fervently and even seek the others' advice, in such a way that they will have to agree that you have to go.

6. Keep cool. It is the mark of superior intelligence and is highly respected. It will show results.

7. Undisciplined discussions in a meeting are common. You may try a joke to call the meeting to order, but in any case, never pass an impolite remark.

8. The general attitude in business is to make a fast buck. If you want to offer your different opinion do it entirely in an objective-oriented way, with plenty of insertions that you, too, can see how wonderful the fast buck would be and how right the others are. Be careful how you introduce future-oriented thinking which is, as yet, rare.

9. Business ethics are loose. If you find a loop, use it.

10. Punctuality is of no value. Being late for an appointment shows that the person is a boss. His esteem rises. Yet punctuality is expected of foreigners.

11. Make sure that you are well protected — in writing — by the boss, the agreement, the deal, etc.

Chapter Ten

ABSORBING THE SHOCK

HOW PAKISTANIS SEE THE FOREIGNER

To the Pakistani, the old caste system of social order is crucially important in assessing a person's merit on a social, business or even marital occasion. It is so important that every form and document mentions caste.

Among the modern city-proletariat these ties are broken. They do not know of caste or clan: they might remember that their grandfather came from such and such area. For people of standing, these are persons of no consequence, neutrals. It is all the more difficult for a Pakistani who has not had exposure abroad to fathom a foreigner. What would be his or her caste? In the absence of more detailed information the nationality of a person has to serve as a caste characteristic which is by nature simplistic.

The media play an important role in establishing the character of a nation, its political alliances and non-alliances, highlighting unusual social behaviour, money machinations and trigger-happy mafias. 85 per cent of the population are illiterate and, though of sound common sense, they listen to the radio and see the world on television open-mouthed. Pakistan is still trying to establish modern cultural foundations. It seeks a helping hand and recognition from almost anywhere in the world. The local press calls a country that gives aid or donations a 'friend' and when the money-flow diminishes, it is no longer a friend. The Pakistani answers the stark realities of international politics with a cry of his emotional and cultural needs: 'Where is the platform on which we can meet? We do not want to be second rate citizens of the world, but you others are running away with the increasing gap between north, south, east and west?' The political, economic and, more so, judicial and cultural struggle for independence and identity is never really taken into account by donor agencies and aid-giving countries. Hence, the Pakistani often reacts negatively in his defensive situation. This has been discussed in the chapter on business but extends to all sectors of life.

The west is both degenerate — just look at the pictures of nudity and sexual behaviour in magazines — and simultaneously it has the last say in matters of scientific thought and progress, and even the continuity of cultural identity. Yet, everybody has between one and five relatives abroad — and those that are left here also want to go.

America

America is the great ideal. Marriage advertisements that include among the applicant's qualities that he is a 'green card holder', i.e., that he is someone who is legally allowed to live and work in the USA, have the greatest chances of finding a partner. It is a love-hate relationship. Americans living in Pakistan keep to themselves, so they are considered arrogant and hypocrites. They represent the implementation of US policy in Pakistan and therefore are often the target of attack when political tempers run high. Everyone here of course wears jeans and drinks coke and has the latest hit record; at the same time they feel inferior because none of these desirable items is made locally. The low income Pakistani also feels a certain class-consciousness when meeting any foreigner. The foreigner's lavish lifestyle causes heartburn to the underpaid clerk as well as to the equally well educated, but also poorly paid, engineer or teacher. The foreigner must always remember that no matter how long he has been in the country he will always be a 'guest' for the people: he is not of any clan, does not share their language, disadvantages, poverty and complexes vis-à-vis the developed world. The Pakistani finds strength in the ties with his equals, or even with his own oppressive overlord.

The German People

You cannot have better credentials than when you can tell that you are a German. The enthusiasm for that country is at times quite embarrassing. The reasons are mostly historic: German products were so good that, earlier this century, the British colonialists found their own trade with — then — India suffering. Consequently, articles bearing the words 'made in Germany' were banned.

For most Pakistanis, Hitler is the greatest hero. They see in him the cause for the freedom of the country from British rule. During World War II, everybody listened into the German radio network and prayed for Hitler's advance through the Khyber Pass. How real that possibility seemed to all is proved by the anti-tank obstructions, the defence posts and bunkers built by the British in the 40 kilometre long pass. Rommel is, for every army officer, the greatest general of all times. It is particularly the martial race of the Pathans that admires the martial qualities of the Germans of those days.

To the Pakistanis, a German woman is virtuous, an excellent housewife and mother, and an economic planner. German modern technology is the last word, but mostly too high-tech and too expensive to be acquired. But as Germans are quite willing to mix with Pakistanis, as they are known — and feared! — to be frank and bluntly outspoken yet appreciative and warm hearted, contacts have apparently been positive and have not changed the traditional image. This image, with tact and understanding, can be preserved on the basis of a more modern reality.

The British

43 years after independence the Pakistani has an ambiguous feeling toward the British: a personal admiration and a political hatred. And, with emotional people this can be spread to any area. It is, for example, a clear indication of the Britishers' ill will, outright sabotage, that they built 800 kilometres of canal system and irrigated the Punjab so that it became the most fertile land of the Sub-continent — but they did not build a drainage system so the same country is now suffering from salinity and water logging, rendering large stretches infertile. Scandalous! Yet under subsequent rulers, I have heard very many people sigh and wish the Britishers were back!

The technical innovations that the British brought with them — railways, hospitals, harbour plants, telecommunication systems and the like together with their honest and remarkably efficient administrative system have had a deep effect on local minds. While some condemn them in general terms, others see it as a means to integrate that period and these happenings in the cultural continuity of the country. Why else should so many men wear western suits? Evidently, the British government had sent their best officers, civilian and military, to the Sub-continent; some have become legendary and books have been written about them. Even though the British fought major wars and innumerably battles against the Pathans, their sentiments for each other bordered on affection.

The British attitude of reserve spells an air of authority, all the more for an emotional people. The British are therefore respected, and interpersonal contacts are polite. Millions of Pakistanis have settled in England since 1947. There, the community relationships are sometimes strained due to economic pressures, but this feeling has not spilled over or affected the feelings of Pakistanis in Pakistan for the British.

Others

The attitude of the Pakistani toward nationals of other western countries is one of 'I don't know you'. Contacts have not been so frequent and beyond the normal hospitable and friendly nature of meetings, the Pakistani has not established a definite relationship of any kind toward them.

Visitors from South-east Asia are met with a kind of reserved friendliness. The Pakistani is aware of a certain difference in their social and cultural background. He respects it and does not question it but also does not show his normal feelings of warmth and enthusiasm. But the Pakistanis are highly appreciative of the modesty of all South-east Asian women. There are quite a number of Pakistanis who have married women from that part of the world.

Pakistanis are, likewise, highly impressed by the Japanese technological progress. Driving along any road in Pakistan you may think you are in Japan; there are few cars other than Japanese ones.

Pakistan has, for decades, maintained a warm political friendship with China. The Chinese are admired for the hard work and efficiency with which they have been, and still are, building their country. In Pakistan, there are families of old Chinese immigrants in every city. They are either artisans or run Chinese restaurants. Both are much visited, but not many friendships have developed. The Chinese here are clan oriented and keep largely to themselves.

People follow the world news with great interest and open mindedness. They have a keen political sense and are usually well informed, often surprisingly so. That, however, does not prevent many people and, worse, the odd post office clerk mixing up Australia with Austria and Brazil with Belgium.

MARRYING A PAKISTANI

This is a very delicate issue and it is difficult to generalise from individual observations. The attitude of the Pakistanis toward a foreign wife is of twofold nature: one group (probably the majority) admires and welcomes her no matter what her nationality is. The other closes their mind to any alliance with the non-Muslim world. This may not be the thinking of the young man who falls in love with a girl abroad, where most mixed marriages arise. But the foreign girl who comes here as a wife must not forget that she is not only married to her husband but to his entire clan. And rejection by his — generally large — family always leads to friction between the couple as the husband is torn between two forces. The bonds of heritage are often the stronger ones.

A frequent situation is that the foreign wife cannot meet the traditional expectations of her mother-in-law and other relatives. Although most families do make allowances for the foreign background of the woman, they nevertheless expect her to learn and adopt the traditional daughter-in-law behaviour, particularly if she is living in the joint family system. She would have to comply with the wishes of her in-laws, particularly of the mother-in-law; she has to accept that her husband is sent on endless errands and duties by his mother and sisters that take him away from her. She has to adjust her life to an entirely different rhythm. It means that she has to give up most of the perspectives a western woman has been brought up with: a job, a career, planning her own day and free time, the western concepts of 'quality of life'. There are women who have achieved it to perfection. They are demure, wear the burquah, have turned Muslim, changed their personalities and devote their lives wholeheartedly to the welfare of the family and clan. A lot depends on the husband: whether he is 'modern' enough to state the limits of 'interference' from his clan.

Most situations involving a foreign wife are not as drastic as the one just described. The situation is much easier if the couple lives alone as is the case in most urban lifestyles. The old mother-in-law may come to live with her son, but the roles are somewhat changed. The wife then can easily go out with her husband while his mother would stay at home. No Pakistani man would like to change Pakistani cooking for western or any other cooking, except for the odd occasion. There, the mother-in-law can prove to be a real boon and sometimes, very loving relationships have developed where both sides meet with understanding and tolerance to accept each other's ways.

Often, it is up to the foreign wife to determine the parameters of social intercourse with her in-laws; among educated families her voice is heard and often respected. If this is accompanied by courtesy toward the elders, an accommodating spirit and readiness to be 'family', the relationships may become very pleasant. The father-in-law is in most cases quite proud when he has a foreign daughter-in-law. Courtesy and perhaps the dupatta over the head is all he may wish for; for most foreign wives take to the Pakistani dress quickly and easily but not all use the dupatta. He normally enjoys a chat with an educated foreign daughter-in-law. He may dictate the son's actions but would not address the daughter-in-law with direct orders.

The Husband

There are husbands who, even when away from their clan, demand all the submissiveness from a foreign wife that they would have received from a Pakistani wife. Some may not be prepared to give up their life with friends in their free time. On the other hand, many Pakistani husbands are fully prepared and even welcome it when their foreign wife takes up a job, limits the number of children even if they should be 'only' girls and is a good hostess to male friends.

How to Make the Best Choice

It is difficult for a young woman brought up in western ways to think of factors of cultural compatibility when she is in love. The girl who wants to marry a Pakistani man who has adopted a western lifestyle must know whether he has done the same back home. There is no guarantee that he can move easily and naturally in this style back home. Men in later years in Pakistan often change and become religious and demand their family to follow the rituals and dogmas of religion as well. Nobody abroad can know during youth whether she later would be able to cope with changing her personality and adopting a new one in order to keep the marriage going.

Other changes in men happen without necessarily adopting a religious way of life. Love marriages with foreign girls often go well for some years in the normal atmosphere of city style living, and sons and daughters are born. The wife may be doing a job and be socially modern and engaged. She may be pretty and well adjusted, normal in all her ways, and admired. Then one day, you hear that the husband has started beating her; stopping her from doing a job; curtailing her social activities; and, on top of it, that he has married a second wife, one that may be from his village and hardly educated. One, or all these things might happen together. The social environment normally condemns the man, and even his own family might side with the foreign woman.

Maybe we can understand why such a thing should happen in the light of what has been said earlier about a Pakistani's feelings about foreign lands and people. When youth and infatuation are over, the overgrown feelings of inadequacy in the face of the consolidated cultural foundations of the wife together with her familiarity with the 'Brave New World' might surface again. A semi-educated village wife will pose no threat to him, so he can relax, and order her to do things according to the old order. If foreign wives decide to leave the country, the situation can become tragic where there are children. Legally, a mother has the right of custody of her sons until they are seven years old, but she has to leave older ones behind. Often, only the sons are claimed by the husband and his family; and the girls may go with the mother.

There are rare cases of Pakistani women marrying foreign men. The men will have to become Muslims before marriage as a Muslim woman is not allowed to marry a non-Muslim. By and large, western men married to women of this part of the world seem to be very happy.

Different Cultures?

Nature, catastrophes and climate, which are extreme environmental forces here, and religion, politics, economics, ethnicity, family and clans as social factors singly or together generate impulses that, often radically, determine our behaviour. Basically, our actions and reactions are the same, only the form differs. And the foreigner who sincerely wishes to be happy in a foreign land needs to understand the basis as well as the form.

The Pakistani, even one of well educated standing, signs an application with 'your most obedient servant XYZ'.This, in spite of several years of budding democracy. He may say to his boss, 'I shall try' but he will not do so, because he actually means 'I cannot do it'. The impact of feudal practices, old or new, coupled with stark economic pressures have pressed him into this attitude of servility. Your new servant will behave likewise, at least initially, until one day, he realises you are not feudal nor of ill-will, and he can look you straight into the eye. Some low grade government servants have developed the permanently round-backed stature of bowing. While foreign ambassadors take part in public plays or play the violin for the entertainment of others, a Pakistani civil servant thinks it below his dignity to answer a telephone call from a person of lower standing. Because the law here is weak, formalism and posture must help to impress and achieve.

The art and fun of bargaining is in the Pakistani's blood, a financial advantage obtained without bargaining is nothing to enjoy. When the salesman quotes you far too high a price and you prepare to leave in protest he calls after you: 'You please quote now,' and means, it is your turn in the game and the dice must be thrown alternately. Play he must, gamble he must, and you must know the game and the rules. Understanding it makes life easier for you here, and you might even begin to enjoy the game yourself.

And when a person does not show you his gratitude for a gift it is because he has been taught that everything comes from God and he must thank Him in his prayer. And that he will do. And when a woman desperately wants offspring and, after intense prayer and many visits to shrines, is blessed with a child and makes the supreme sacrifice — for a westerner, a horrible sacrifice — of giving her first born male child to the religious group of the shrine she does the same as a Catholic who lights a candle in the church; only, her sacrifice is so much more sublime for her sufferings over it.

Signs of Clash

For some foreigners the different way of living comes as a great shock. They react either by encapsulation or flight. Both reactions show a failure to adjust to the new environment. The encapsulated foreigner largely withdraws from social intercourse with Pakistanis and spends his or her free time in the company of his compatriots or other foreigners of his cultural background. The result is that he or she is the loser. He cannot mix: so he cannot learn to understand and consequently, cannot appreciate the things, matters and people of his host country. When a foreigner's conversation with you is dominated by 'these people here, why must they be so rude? Why can't he tell me straight?' he is likewise on the encapsulation track that brings him nowhere nearer happiness or even business success.

The other sufferer from culture shock will try to get his contract cancelled or shortened, and pack up and leave. Persons who cannot assert themselves well in their own culture really feel the vacuum of organised public fun and performances. For some expatriates, the availability or non-availability of scotch and beer is the criterion of their like or dislike for the country. They are often people who do not really seek the contact with, and understanding of, the country.

Young people often express the urgent desire to leave. For them, there is 'no life here': no discos, no excitement, no extrovert 'normal' showing of fondness, no elegance, boring TV, no laughter. It's true enough, but all these things exist, in the privacy of a Pakistani friend's home. In every big city there are lots of Pakistani boys and girls who regularly meet in homes for disco dancing, fun and laughter. The ball is in your court: go out and meet them, it's not difficult!

PREPARATIONS

The visitor needs to do two things: from the moment he knows that he is going abroad he must convince himself that his environment there will definitely be different from the one of his home country. Secondly, he must actively prepare for it. Far from your destination, the easiest way to acquaint yourself with your future environment is to read. Get material from libraries, from consulates and tourist offices. By reading you make the first step towards the place that may be your chosen holiday spot or your home for a few years. When, on the aircraft, you can tell your co-traveller next to you that you are just flying over the Indus you have completed a big step, because you know. Knowing makes you feel at home.

The same goes for the people: when you understand them you automatically draw close to them. It is your own efforts, your preparations, the words of the language you have learnt to communicate better, that determine the degree of your cultural well-being in the host country. When it is you who can explain to another expatriate that, by saying 'family', Mr X means his wife since his social background is such that he is too shy to use the name of his wife, you are comfortably on the way to being at home in Pakistan.

The people of Pakistan are culturally most assertive in terms of their religion and ethnic background. Both use symbols of centuries ago. Not many new ones have been added in the turmoil of conquests and under colonial rule. Also, the religious expressions of culture, largely absorbed in a huge body of 'customs and traditions' are so forceful that it is difficult to find new, creative avenues of cultural expression. That is why a Pakistani looks backwards for solace, guidance and truth and to the glorious moments of the country — centuries old; and hardly ever to the future.

The Clash Within

If you feel depressed by culture shock, it's perhaps helpful to remember that many Pakistanis feel and suffer from the same clash and much more so than you. It is the intellectuals, the creative thinkers, the social reformers and economic developers who not only plead for change but often live a schizophrenic life, and are torn between two worlds. The youth picks up his beauty queen from a magazine, but his sisters and mother live in purdah. Advertisements show emancipated, beautiful women, racy cars and boat-joy-rides with coke in mixed, laughing company while by his upbringing, he is not supposed to look at women and forgo the worldliness of loud and laughing joy. He seeks self-expression, but his marks in the examination will be cut if he uses phrases or ideas that are not contained in the textbooks. The examples are endless. And he cannot even fall back for assurance to another culture as you can — to your own, which is your culture shock absorber.

Your Shock Absorber in Operation

You might explain to a Pakistani why a gentleman gets up when a lady enters, if you can. The foreign gentleman's behaviour may show that the west is not really as decadent as it is made to be. Above all, remain gentle. As Coleridge said 'Advice is like snow; the softer it falls the deeper it sinks into the mind.' A young man is often so very grateful for a word of advice which is in tune with reality. Often, he does not get that at home where the ego of the elders dominates or he hears phrases like 'God will help' which leave him high and dry. You might show him how to take the initiative or practical action which is something that few have yet learnt to do.

It is high time that the West created a stronger cultural image in Pakistan. For the more aid that flows into the country, the more depressing it is for the people psychologically. Each positive gesture of yours is important. And with it, you create a situation of your own and lend it your cultural impact. From this position of strength you should be patient enough to hear and accept the other's response — and without being patronising.

It is mostly on small issues that the sting of cultural differences is felt in daily life: the lack of punctuality, unreliability, enthusiastic promises broken, the concept of 'tomorrow', dishonest deals and bargains, and in business ethics. Often, you resign yourself to it and accept what you alone cannot change. But do not condemn, as the people, even in such actions, live out their own truth. Some day, they might know better. For a while Pakistan has not been able to sell inferior products on the international markets. But the new truth, to make better ones, has dawned on only a few.

Can East Meet West?

This question is perhaps more topical now than ever before. Up until the age of the rifle, the person of the Sub-continent was able to keep pace with the west in his mental reality. He understood a rifle. But the age of the spaceship, of the computer and genetic engineering has left him hopelessly behind and, in his mind, he is building up a position of confrontation. The gap is felt acutely. There is hardly an article of the kind of critical appreciation in the press that does not include: '... even in the west this is done so ...' which turns the west into an unrealised ideal. But also: '... due to imperialist machinations of the West (we were left behind)...'. This does not augur well for east-west relations in its psychological implications.

It is in the world of institutions, technological advancement, critical and philosophical thought that this gap is widening. In a person to person relationship there should hardly be any problem. Think of the differences within the European Community: there you have the stiff, formal, heavy-set and contemplative north European next to the singing swinging Italian. Yet, there is integration. In World War II my aunt cried herself blind over the loss of her fortune while a friend, similarly affected, thanked God that he was alive. One person sees that the glass is half full, the other sees that it is half empty. You have all the shock absorbers within you: use them.

CULTURE SHOCK
ADJUSTMENT TABLE

Adjustments to a new environment happen slowly. If you come with positive intentions for your new life or the holidays you want to spend in the country, they will seep into you unawares.

The table is meant to help you analyse what strides you have made since your arrival. To what extent would you react in the way stated to the following situations? Each question shows the highest achievable score. Be your own judge. Use a pencil for writing your scores and erase them later so that others can also use the list.

1. When at 45° C the electricity stops under the load-shedding economy programme and you drip like an ice-cream in a sauna, hot air comes out of your ears, every spoon you touch is hot, your clothes stick with every step; when you wake up ten times in a night because your neck is bathed in sweat and you say, 'I am glad to be here! I always wanted to be out of the cold of my country and in a land where sunshine is guaranteed! How delightful the bare floor feels under my bare feet! And a cold drink has never been so delicious in my life!'   (4)

2. When you can eat spicy food or fruit in the bazaar straight from the vendor's cart or counter without any negative effects on your digestive system.   (3)

3. When the mullah's voice over the loudspeaker system at 3.30 in the morning no longer wakes you up — or, if awoken, you turn to the other side and decide to sleep on.   (3)

4. When you become aware that the humble artisan lives a life much more in consonance with cultural traditions than many well-to-do or highly placed persons or friends of yours in urban society.   (3)

5. When you, a lady, discover the virtues of local dress and wear it when you go out (at least).   (3)

6. When you no longer think and say 'these people' and you bristle with embarrassment when you hear other foreigners use the terms.   (3)

7. When you stop seeing things and people from a visitor's angle and stop saying 'Oh, he was so interesting!' after a meeting with a local person.   (3)

8. When you can sit through a 3-hour music recital cross legged on the ground on the carpet. (1)

9. When your nose no longer gets alarmed over the spicy and sweet odours or their opposite in the bazaars. (2)

10. When you do not sit with your husband/wife/sweetheart in the familiar pose of affectionate closeness in the drawing room. (2)

11. When you see a woman in purple shalwar, blue kamis and green dupatta and you don't wince. (2)

12. When the burquah-clad woman in the street no longer strikes you as something abnormal but is a normal part of the street scene for you. (3)

13. When, as a housewife, you no longer exclaim 'Oh, yet again the servant hasn't done this or that or, Again he messed up this or that' but instead, before anything else in the morning, tell him precisely what and where to dust, what to cook and what spices to omit, etc. (3)

14. When, in a conversation, you do not compare your guestland with your homeland and highlight the better conditions and advantages of the latter. (1)

15. When you can accept the truth of 'Sorry, I could not come to your dinner last night. A visitor dropped in and I could not even inform you as the telephone was right there where we sat; it would have been discourteous. I hope I did not cause you any inconvenience'—the truth in terms of his reality. (3)

16. When you understand that 'Yes Sir' in some situations may mean 'No, sorry' and accept it gracefully without thinking the person is a liar. (2)

17. When you, upon hearing the word 'yes, soon', are able to stretch your mind to anticipate any length of time up to a maximum of a couple of years. (2)

18. When you drive your car and find that most other cars are trying to show you that they can drive faster — and keep your cool. (3)

19. When you can sit through a 5-hour wedding ceremony and still find it charming. (2)

20. When you see poverty and squalid living conditions and think: 'How bravely they are living with it!' (2)

ACHIEVEMENT TABLE

50 points: maximum score. Adjustment achieved. Keep it up!

40–50 points: You are almost there and will feel no pinch trying a little more.

30–40 points: You are on the way but need to try harder. Beware of negative thinking.

20–30 points: You are definitely faced with a problem of adjustment. You need to analyse your own actions and reactions closely along with that of your environment. At your leisure, read through the book.

10-20 points: You need to ask yourself why you are in the country; why is it that others feel happy here and you do not; do you really have to stay on or is it worth it to try to live a more fulfilled life elsewhere?

10-0 points: Give yourself one month and do the test again. If your score does not improve you need to think of changing your life: go elsewhere, or radically examine your thinking on human life and your expectations.

CULTURAL QUIZ

We are sure you have gone through the book carefully and understood what it means to convey. Still, how can you be sure you follow the suggestions and advice given here? You will certainly make many mistakes in the beginning — and learn from them.

The cultural quiz is meant to focus on your achievements or point out your failures. Award the marks yourself and you become your own judge of your correct or incorrect actions. You are bound to remember it when you are in this or a similar situation again.

SITUATION 1

You are in a handicraft shop. The shopkeeper tells you a highly exaggerated price. How do you react correctly?

A   Leave the shop.
B   Bargain.
C   Raise your voice in protest.
D   Answer sarcastically.
E   Teach him a lesson by threatening to warn your friends.

Highest score: +5
Answer: *A*: 0; *B*: +5; *C*: 0; *D*: –3; *E*: –2

Comments

Remember that bargaining is a game, a gamble, by which the salesman can show his skill and challenge yours. If you deny it to him, he would feel that you had not given him a chance to elucidate his sales points. Therefore he would look at you blankly if you answer sarcastically or threaten him. And as to raising your voice — it's not the behaviour of a gentleman. Leaving the shop means to him that you have given up or you are not genuinely interested.

SITUATION 2: (Several Possible Scores)

You are seated in a carpet shop. Bargaining has started. How should you conduct it and what responses are due?

A   Find fault with the item.

B   Show a commercial smile to obtain a favour.

C   Beg.

D   Explain you are not so well off.

E   Promise to come for more shopping and to bring friends along.

F   Pretend to leave.

G   Try again the next day.

H   Bring a local friend along.

Highest score: +10

Answer: *A*: –3; *B*: 0; *C*: +1; *D*: +1; *E*: +3 *F*: +4 *G*: 0; *H*: +4

Comments

To find fault with an item where there is none is too common a behaviour and is not considered a genuine reason. A commercial

smile might work, but might also be felt as not inter-personal but 'commercial'. If you beg, and request with sincerity to appeal to his kindness, you establish a kind of personal relationship and might profit in a small way. If you, upon being shown several items persistently reject the expensive ones as being beyond your means, you might also get a small advantage — or he might show you cheaper items. If you frequent the shop and, upon an offer in your favour, promise to come again and bring other friends along, the trust that you have established will work in your favour. If you get up with a sigh of regret and move towards the door, the speed of reduced rates from the mouth of the salesman will remind you of the ball in roulette; you may then settle back for a new round of negotiations. Just trying again another day mostly leads to nothing. Bringing a local along might work in your favour if you are sure that the salesman is a tradition-conscious, religious Pakistani who will listen to the pleas of a compatriot. If he is a dollar-conscious and foreigner-seeking person, it would misfire.

SITUATION 3

Tempting smells of roast chicken, sweet cakes and spicy titbits make you slow down your step and make you think, 'Shouldn't I try it? When all others eat it, why can't I?'

The table includes some 'No's' for the potently dangerous temptations; a 'later' to allow for adjustments and the experienced traveller; and a 'yes' for eats and drinks that are harmless — but you need to decide yourself whether there could have been a possibility of a fly having penetrated to the otherwise well covered and clean looking food or drink of your fancy:

A Cakes and biscuits from a good bakery.
B Bananas, oranges, apples, nuts.
C Tea.
D A samosa.
E Local sweets (mit'hia'i).

F   Meat on skewers.
G   Roti of all kinds.
H   Bottled drink.
I   Open drink.
J   Freshly extracted juices.
K   Lassi.
L   Chat.
M   Kebab.
N   Curry from a cheap open restaurant.
I   Apples (with peel)

Highest score: 15
Answer: A: Yes; B: Yes; C: Yes; D: No; E: Later; F: Later;
G: Yes; H: Yes; I No; J: Later; K: Later; L No; M No; N:
No; O: Later

Comments

Everything which is baked is clean and all foreigners buy it. Peeled
fruit is also safe for you. Tea is fine as the water has been boiled
over a prolonged time. Samosas, though absolutely delicious, do not
always contain a fresh or hygenically prepared filling. The local
sweets might contain too much sugar for your stomach. They also
attract flies quickly and in plenty. Meat on skewers, if prepared and
packed before your eyes, is safe; but the spices often cause problems for the newcomer. Roti is an emphatic 'yes'. Bottled drinks of
the international makes are all right for you, while you cannot be
sure of the ingredients of the open drinks sold from vessels or cans.
Freshly extracted juices of peeled fruit (also of carrots) in the bazaar
should be resisted for some time. The glasses are often not washed
in really clean water, and juice is sometimes diluted with water.
Lassi, the sun-stroke preventive sour-milk drink, might cause a
loose stomach for the newcomer. Chats are dangerous because of
flies and spices. And you never really know what a kebab (mince

meat on skewers or done in the pan) contains. The same goes for curries from a bazaar-type restaurant. Unpeeled apples are quite safe from a dealer's tray if you rub or wash them well and from experience know how your stomach will react.

Make sure that plate, spoon and glass are clean or have them washed before your eyes. When bottled drinks are taken heavily chilled, they may cause great trouble for you.

SITUATION 4: (Several scores)

You are accosted by beggars. What is the best thing to do in order to make them leave?

A   Turn about harshly.
B   Tell them to do honest work.

C   Give them a one rupee note.

D   Say a clear and polite 'NO'.

E   Be abusive or show disdain.

F   Gesture them to go if they persist.

Highest score: +5

Answer: *A*: –3; *B*: –5; *C* +5; *D*: +3; *E*: –5; *F* +2

Comments

When you turn your back on a beggar he generally comes around from the other side. If you think that by telling him about 'honest work' you have done a good job in improving his morals, you will be disappointed by his bland eyes. For the poor, any job that brings in money is good. If you want to see them leave quickly, hand them a rupee note or two. Saying a polite 'no' will still keep them hanging around but, at the same time, looking for other sources around you. They are immune to abuse, they cannot comprehend why you should behave thus. Mostly they leave if you continue shaking your head or keep your hand waving.

SITUATION 5: (Several Possible Scores)

A Pakistani invites you to a meal that is in progress. For whatever reason you do not want to eat. How will you answer him?

A   I have already eaten.

B   It's too spicy/greasy.

C   I am on a diet.

D   I have a bad stomach and the doctor allowed me only plain tea.

Highest score: +7

Answer:*A*: +2; *B:* 3; *C*: –2; *D:* +5

Comments

With the first answer you might be forced to accept one piece of roti as symbolic gesture of having shared the meal. To say it is too spicy or greasy would be considered rude as it contains criticism. A diet would not be accepted as a valid excuse, for hospitality is a noble concept which you do not abuse by something as absurd, unimportant and strange as a diet. But the ruling of a doctor is a valid excuse.

SITUATION 6: (Several Possible Scores)

At a conference you find that the company boss does not share your expert view of a given problem. How will you tackle the situation to save the project while at the same time preserving your expert-image and the boss's ego?

A   Express your opinion emphatically during the conference.

B   Explain that the boss's point of view is not helpful.

C   Explain your view to the boss prior to the conference and make it clear to him that you would press your point — and then act on it.

D   Discuss your opinion prior to and with other members of the conference possibly at a social meeting.

E   See the boss after the conference and tell him that his opinion
       is of no advantage to the project.
F   Reconsider and find other options in the light of opposition
       by others.

Highest score: +10
Answer: *A*: +1; *B*: -4; *C*: +3; *D*: +3; *E*: -1; *F*: +3

Comments

With *A* as an answer you might score with the support of other
participants, but the boss would probably not like it. Your relationship with him (and therefore, your success in the company) would
suffer badly if you adopted answer *B*. With *C* and *D* you have a
tactical and psychological advantage. Option *E* would mean that the
boss had already viewed his wrong opinion and would suffer loss of
face if he now changed it. Option *F* can be either useful or an easy
way out if your professional integrity will not suffer by it.

SITUATION 7

Very often you have a dinner commitment or official engagement and your neighbour or friends drop in. How do you make it clear to them that, after ten minutes of chatting, you have to be off?

A   Sorry, but I have to go now.

B   I am in a hurry; can I give you a lift?

C   I have a spot of work at the office. May I leave you in the care of my family? I shall be back very quickly.

D   We have an important engagement right now. I hate to interrupt this interesting conversation; can you make it for dinner tomorrow so that we continue it?

Highest score: +8
Answer: *A:* – 4; *B:* –1; *C:* +3; *D:* +5

Comments

Remember that hospitality is one of the highest cultural values! *A* would be an abrupt and discourteous 'good riddance' which might even cancel social relationships.(Others, mostly professionals, will show more understanding.) In answer *B* the shock would only be mildly compensated by the offer of a lift. Answer *C* works well if you can convince the person of the urgency of your commitment which is normally accepted. *D* is of course tradition- and culture-conscious and proves you as a gentleman. And you are tactically at an advantage as the ball is now in the court of the other party.

SITUATION 8

You are going somewhere in your car and out of the blue, a police-man stops you and demands to see your documents. You sense that he is a person who is under culture shock vis-à-vis a foreigner. What will you do to prevent a scene and finish the interview quickly?

A   Show him your papers.

B   Refuse to show him your papers.

C   Smile, fumble, explain.

D   Speak Urdu.

E   Speak English.

F   Ask him his rank and the purpose of stopping you for nothing, with a cool air of authority.

G   Show a behaviour that reveals fear of or submission to a uniform.

H   Offer him money.

Highest score: +10

Answer: A: +5; B:–3; C: –3; D: –2; E: +2; F +3; G: – 2;H: 0

Comments

You are socially at an advantage. You must show that although you appreciate correctness you will stand no nonsense. To pass money might end the scene quickly but could also misfire.

SITUATION 9

You are receiving guests for dinner, reception or party.

A: Do you (a male) uninvited shake hands with a lady-guest?
   (i) Yes   (ii) No

B: Do you (a lady) shake hands with a male Pakistani guest?
   (i) Yes   (ii) No

Highest score: +2

Answer: A: (i) –1;   (ii) +1   B: (i) +1   (ii) –1

Comments

Remember that your social conduct with ladies (unless they are real friends) must be formal. If she desires a handshake, she will offer

you her hand and you accept it with some pleasant words. A foreign lady may easily offer her hand to a male guest. But she should still be prepared that for many men, this is a surprise that they are not used to. The handshake may be a disappointment in this case.

ABOUT THE AUTHORS

Karin Mittmann hails from Berlin in Germany. She married a Pakistani in 1955. After the dissolution of her marriage she stayed on in the country as it was the choice of her children. She has been teaching at the universities of Peshawar and Islamabad. After her daughters were married, she resigned and began to teach privately in order to have more time for creative work and writing. She has since published a volume of poetry and many articles. A volume of prose is currently going to press.

Zafar Ihsan is the son of a retired doctor who worked for the Pakistan Railways. Since his father was transferred to innumerable stations, Zafar has lived in all four provinces of the country and gained a deep insight into the thinking and problems of the people and their lifestyles. He is a systems analyst and works and lives in Karachi. He is Karin Mittmann's son-in-law.

Akhtar Shah joined the English daily newspaper *The Muslim* in Islamabad as a cartoonist after ten years' experience in other centres. In keeping with his artistic temperament, he spends times of financial and creative depression fishing in the Rawal Lake or climbing mountains where nature brings him solace and inspiration.

FURTHER READING

These are just some of the books I have found enjoyable, giving a wider perspective on the history, sociology and culture of Pakistan.

The Old Classics: 19th Century to Partition (1947)

Travels into Bokhara (3 volume cassette). Alexander Burns, Oxford University Press.

The Pathans. Sir Olaf Cairo, Oxford University Press. The all-time classic of historical/socio/cultural studies.

Moghul Glory. M. Lal, Vanguard.

Narrative of Various Journeys in Balochistan, Afghanistan and the Punjab. Charles Masson, Oxford University Press.

Among the Wild Tribes of the Afghan Frontier. T. L. Pennel, Oxford University Press.

18 Years in the Khyber 1879–98. Sir Robert Warbourton, Oxford University Press.

Post-Partition Books on Pakistan

Pakistan — The Social Sciences. Akbar S. Ahmad (Ed.), Oxford University Press. A sociological study.

Pakistan Society. Akbar S. Ahmad, Oxford University Press. A socio-cultural study.

Freedom at Midnight. Collins/Lapierre, Avon. A fascinating pre- and post-partition historical description.

The North-West Frontier of West Pakistan. David Dichter, Clarendon, 1970. A socio-historical treatment.

Breaking the Curfew: Political Journey Through Pakistan. Emma Duncan, Michael Joseph. A post-partition political history.

Pakistan in the Pamir Knot. Zulfiqar Khalid, Vanguard. An angle of geopolitical imperatives.

Friends not Masters. Ayub Khan, President of Pakistan.

Women's Seclusion and Men's Honour. David Mandelbaum, Oxford. Socio-critical.

Travels in Baluchistan and Sind. Henry Pottinger, Indus Publications, Karachi. Socio-political.

Jinnah of Pakistan. Stanley Wolpert, Oxford.

The Last Wali of Swat(Autobiography). Oxford. Memoirs of the last ruler of the Kingdom of Swat.

Travels, Guides and Accounts

The Silk Road. Judy Bonaviq, Collins.

The Lion-River, the Indus. Jean Fairley, S. I. Gilani, Lahore.

Where the Indus is Young (A Winter in Baltistan). Dervla Murphy, John Murray, 1977. Northern travels.

Illustrated Guide to Pakistan. Isobel Shaw, The Guidebook Co.

Pakistan Handbook. Isobel Shaw, Oxford. This and the *Illustrated Guide* are the best handbooks currently on the market.

The Trekker's Guide to the Himalayas and Karakorum. Hugh Swift, Hodder & Stoughton.

Books for the Inquisitive

The Rags of North Indian Music. N.A. Jairazbhoy, Lok Viersa, Islamabad. Classical music.

A Morning in the Wilderness. Waqas A. Khwaja (Ed.), Sang-e-Meel, Lahore. Selected poetry and short stories.

Archaeological Guide to Taxila. John Marshall, Jodhpur 1918, 1986.

Oriental Rugs. John K. Mumford, Bramhall House, New York.

Harappan Civilization & Rojdi. G.L. Possehl, Oxford.

A History of Urdu Literature. Ram Babu Sahzma, Sind Sagar Academy, Lahore.

Calligraphy and Islamic Culture. Annemarie Schimmel, New York University Press.

The Crow Eaters. Bapsi Sidhwa, Fontana/Collins. Novel.

ACKNOWLEDGEMENTS

The authors would like to express their warmest thanks to Professor Annemarie Schimmel who was a source of inspiration and who took the trouble to read through the text giving valuable comments and suggestions.

They are also grateful to Mr Mohammad Ashraf in whose office they found valuable typing assistance whenever their typewriter was silenced by the rigours of load-shedding.

The authors and publishers would like to thank the Director, Pakistan Tourism Development Corporation of the Ministry of Tourism, as well as the Director, Films and Publications of the Ministry of Information for their help in providing photographs. Thanks too, to Mr. G.G. Raza for making some of his excellent photographs available for this publication.

INDEX